Inside Reading

THE ACADEMIC WORD LIST IN CONTEXT

By Bruce Rubin

with Denise Maduli-Williams and Lara M. Ravitch

Series Director: Cheryl Boyd Zimmerman

3

OXFORD
UNIVERSITY PRESS

OXFORD
UNIVERSITY PRESS

198 Madison Avenue
New York, NY 10016 USA

Great Clarendon Street, Oxford OX2 6DP UK

Oxford University Press is a department of the University of Oxford.
It furthers the University's objective of excellence in research, scholarship,
and education by publishing worldwide in

Oxford New York

Auckland Cape Town Dar es Salaam Hong Kong Karachi
Kuala Lumpur Madrid Melbourne Mexico City Nairobi
New Delhi Shanghai Taipei Toronto

With offices in

Argentina Austria Brazil Chile Czech Republic France Greece
Guatemala Hungary Italy Japan Poland Portugal Singapore
South Korea Switzerland Thailand Turkey Ukraine Vietnam

OXFORD and OXFORD ENGLISH are registered trademarks of
Oxford University Press.

© Oxford University Press 2009

Database right Oxford University Press (maker)

Library of Congress Cataloging-in-Publication Data
Burgmeier, Arline
    Inside reading 1: the academic word list in context / Arline Burgmeier.
        p. cm.
    ISBN 978-0-19-441612-2 (pbk. w/ cdrom)
    1. English language—Textbooks for foreign speakers. 2. Vocabulary. I. Title.
    PE1128.B846 2007
    428.2'4—dc22   2007023406

No unauthorized photocopying.

All rights reserved. No part of this publication may be reproduced,
stored in a retrieval system, or transmitted, in any form or by any means,
without the prior permission in writing of Oxford University Press,
or as expressly permitted by law, or under terms agreed with the appropriate
copyright clearance organization. Enquiries concerning reproduction outside
the scope of the above should be sent to the ELT Rights Department, Oxford
University Press, at the address above.

You must not circulate this book in any other binding or cover
and you must impose this same condition on any acquirer.

Any websites referred to in this publication are in the public domain and
their addresses are provided by Oxford University Press for information only.
Oxford University Press disclaims any responsibility for the content.

Editorial Director: Sally Yagan
Senior Managing Editor: Patricia O'Neill
Editor: Dena Daniel
Design Director: Robert Carangelo
Design Manager: Maj-Britt Hagsted
Production Artist: Julie Armstrong
Compositor: TSI Graphics Inc.
Cover design: Stacy Merlin
Manufacturing Manager: Shanta Persaud
Manufacturing Controller: Zai Jawat Ali

Student book pack ISBN: 978 0 19 441614 6
Student book ISBN: 978 0 19 441606 1

Printed in Hong Kong

10 9 8 7 6 5 4 3 2

ACKNOWLEDGMENTS

The publisher would like to thank TSI Graphics for the illustrations used in this book.

The publisher would like to thank the following for their permission to reproduce photographs: Courtesy of the Library of Congress, LC-G612- 54612: 3; G.E. Kidder Smith/Corbis: 4; ALIKI SAPOUNTZI/aliki image library/Alamy: 35; Blank Archives/Getty Images: 43; AP Photo/Mel Evans:43; Dartfish Stromotion: 66; Eadweard Muybridge/Time Life Pictures/Getty Images: 73; Courtesy of the Library of Congress, LC-USZ62-50927: 83; Yvette Cardozo/Jupiter Images: 88; Vic Bider/Jupiter Images: 90; Medical-on-Line / Alamy: 105; AP Photo/The Tennessean, Rex Perry: 114; The Granger Collection, New York: 130; The Granger Collection, New York: 131; Nowosti - ullstein bild / The Granger Collection: 131; Deborah Feingold/Corbis: 131; Bill Inoshita/CBS Photo Archive/ Getty Images: 132; Michael Ventura / Alamy: 147

Cover art: The Image Works: Lee Snider (Cow Parade); Brand X / Age FotoStock: (Sextant).

The publisher would like to thank the following for their permission to reproduce copyrighted material: **pp. 3–4**, "The Terrazzo Jungle," by Malcolm Gladwell, *The New Yorker*, March 15, 2004. Reprinted and adapted with permission. **pp. 10–11**, Adapted from The Mills Corporation, "Press Release #2: Architects," 1956 grand Opening press release. **pp. 18–19**, Adapted from Newsweek International, "The New Megalopolis," July 3, 2006. **pp. 25–26**, "Ecopolis Now," by Fred Pearce, *New Scientist*, June 17, 2006. Reprinted and adapted with permission. **pp. 35–36**, "The Best of Moonicipal Art," *The Scotsman*, May 13, 2006. Reprinted and adapted with permission. **pp. 43–45**, "Going to the Dogs… And cows and pigs and horses? The trend in public art has been a boon to many communities, and a source of dismay for many in the fine arts," by Thomas Vinciguerra, October 5, 2005, © 2006 by *The Philadelphia Inquirer*. Reprinted and adapted with permission. **pp. 50–52**, "The Determinants of Mortality," by David Cutler, Angus Deaton, and Adriana Lleras-Muney, *Journal of Economic Perspectives* (Vol 20, Number 3, Summer 2006). Adapted and reprinted with permission of the authors and the American Economic Association. **p. 50**, Figure 1, "World Infant Mortality Rates, 1950-2005," Worldwatch Institute. Reprinted with permission. **p. 51**, Figure 2, "Chlorination, Clean Water and the Public Health Progress that Changed America," Water Quality and Health Council, Reprinted with permission. **p. 51**, Figure 3, "The State of the World's Children 2003," Unicef. Reprinted with permission. **pp. 57–59**, The Benefits of Immunization, World Health Organization, Switzerland (http://www.who.int/mediacentre/factsheets/ fs288/en/). Reprinted and adapted with permission. **p. 57**, Tables 1 and 2, UNICEF. Reprinted with permission. **p. 60**, pie chart, "Vaccine-Preventable Diseases," World Health Organization. Reprinted with permission. **pp. 66–67**, "The Dartfish Olympics," by Clive Thompson. © 2007 by Clive Thompson. Reprinted and adapted with permission. **p. 67**, "BBC Sport uses StroMotion technique for first time in UK," BBC press release. **pp. 90–91**, Adapted from "Are Amusement Park Thrill Rides Lethal?" *Popular Mechanics*, August 2003. **pp. 99–101**, Adapted from a book review of Steven Johnson's *Mind Wide Open*, by Jonathan Weiner, *The New York Times*, May 9, 2004. **pp. 105–108**, "Out-of-Body Experience? Your Brain Is to Blame," by Sandra Blakeslee, *The New York Times*, October 3, 2006. Copyright © 2006 by The New York Times Co. Reprinted and adapted with permission. **pp. 121–122**, Adapted from "How to Raise a Genius," by Nicholas Weinstock, *The New York Times*, November 10, 2005. **pp. 130–132**, Adapted from "Personal Best: Timeline," *BusinessWeek*, August 21/28, 2006. **pp. 138–139**, Adapted from "Type A Organizations: Timeline," and "Management Grab," *BusinessWeek*, August 21/28, 2006. **pp. 146–148**, "Getting There: The Science of Driving Directions," by Nick Paumgarten, *The New Yorker*, April 24, 2006. Adapted and reprinted with permission. **pp. 152–155**, Adapted from Wikipedia.com entry for "navigation."

Acknowledgments

From the Series Director

Inside Reading represents collaboration as it should be. That is, the project resulted from a balance of expertise from a team at Oxford University Press (OUP) and a collection of skilled participants from several universities. The project would not have happened without considerable investment and talent from both sides.

This idea took root and developed with the collaboration and support of the OUP editorial team. I am particularly grateful to Pietro Alongi, whose vision for this series began with his recognition of the reciprocal relationship between reading and vocabulary. I am also grateful to Dena Daniel, the lead editor on the project, and Janet Aitchison for her involvement in the early stages of this venture.

OUP was joined by the contributions of participants from various academic settings. First, Averil Coxhead, Massey University, New Zealand, created the Academic Word List, a principled, research-based collection of academic words which has led both to much of the research which supports this project and to the materials themselves. Dr. Tom Klammer, Dean of Humanities and Social Sciences at California State University, Fullerton (CSUF), made my participation in this project possible, first by endorsing its value, then by providing the time I needed. Assistance and insight were provided by CSUF participants Patricia Balderas, Arline Burgmeier, and Margaret Plenert, as well as by many TESOL Masters students at CSUF.

Finally, thank you to the many reviewers who gave us feedback along the way: Nancy Baum, **University of Texas at Arlington**; Adele Camus, **George Mason University**; Carole Collins, **Northampton Community College**; Jennifer Farnell, **University of Connecticut**, ALP; Laurie Frazier, **University of Minnesota**; Debbie Gold, **California State University**, Long Beach, ALI; Janet Harclerode and Toni Randall, **Santa Monica Community College**; Marianne Hsu Santelli, **Middlesex County College**; Steve Jones, **Community College of Philadelphia**; Lucille King, **University of Connecticut**; Shalle Leeming, **Academy of Art University**, San Francisco; Gerry Luton, **University of Victoria**; David Mindock, **University of Denver**; William Morrill, **University of Washington**; and Peggy Alptekin. This is collaboration indeed!

From the Author

I am very grateful to Pietro Alongi and to Dena Daniel of Oxford University Press for their graciousness and diligence in directing the creation of this book. I would also like to offer a big thanks to Cheryl Zimmerman for being a super supportive colleague and longtime trusty vocabulary-teaching guide. In addition, I would like to extend my deep appreciation to all of my colleagues at California State University, Fullerton, and the North Orange County School of Continuing Education for their ongoing generosity and professionalism.

Contents

Unit 1 **The Birth of the Mall**   1

Content area: Architecture

Unit 2 **Megacities**   17

Content area: Urban Planning

Unit 3 **In the Public Eye**   33

Content area: Art & Design

Unit 4 **Staying Alive**   49

Content area: Public Health

Unit 5 **Bodies in Motions**   65

Content area: Film Studies

To the Teacher

There is a natural relationship between academic reading and word learning. *Inside Reading* is a four-level reading and vocabulary series designed to use this relationship to best advantage. Through principled instruction and practice with reading strategies and skills, students will increase their ability to comprehend reading material. Likewise, through a principled approach to the complex nature of vocabulary knowledge, learners will better understand how to make sense of the complex nature of academic word learning. *Inside Reading 3* is intended for students at the high-intermediate level.

Academic Reading and Vocabulary: A Reciprocal Relationship

In the beginning stages of language learning, when the learner is making simple connections between familiar oral words and written forms, vocabulary knowledge plays a crucial role. In later stages, such as those addressed by *Inside Reading*, word learning and reading are increasingly interdependent: rich word knowledge facilitates reading, and effective reading skills facilitate vocabulary comprehension and learning.[1]

The word knowledge that is needed by the reader in this reciprocal process is more than knowledge of definitions.[2] Truly knowing a word well enough to use it in reading (as well as in production) means knowing something about its grammar, word forms, collocations, register, associations, and a great deal about its meaning, including its connotations and multiple meanings.[3] Any of this information may be called upon to help the reader make the inferences needed to understand the word's meaning in a particular text. For example, a passage's meaning can be controlled completely by a connotation

She was *frugal*. (positive connotation)

She was *stingy*. (negative connotation)

by grammatical form

He valued his *memory*.

He valued his *memories*.

or an alternate meaning

The *labor* was intense. (physical work vs. childbirth)

Inside Reading recognizes the complexity of knowing a word. Students are given frequent and varied practice with all aspects of word knowledge. Vocabulary activities are closely related in topic to the reading selections, providing multiple exposures to a word in actual use and opportunities to work with its meanings, grammatical features, word forms, collocations, register, and associations.

To join principled vocabulary instruction with academic reading instruction is both natural and effective. *Inside Reading* is designed to address the reciprocal relationship between reading and vocabulary and to use it to help students develop academic proficiency.

A Closer Look at Academic Reading

Students preparing for academic work benefit from instruction that includes attention to the language as well as attention to the process of reading. The Interactive Reading model indicates that reading is an active process in which readers draw upon *top-down processing* (bringing meaning to the text), as well as *bottom-up processing* (decoding words and other details of language).[4]

The *top-down* aspect of this construct suggests that reading is facilitated by interesting and relevant reading materials that activate a range of knowledge in a reader's mind, knowledge that is refined and extended during the act of reading.

The *bottom-up* aspect of this model suggests that the learner needs to pay attention to language proficiency, including vocabulary. An academic reading course must address the teaching of higher-level reading strategies without neglecting the need for language support.[5]

---

[1] Koda, 2005

[2] See the meta-analysis of L1 vocabulary studies by Stahl & Fairbanks, 1986.

[3] Nation, 1990

[4] Carrell, Devine, and Eskey, 1988

[5] Birch, 2002; Eskey, 1988

Inside Reading addresses both sides of the interactive model. High-interest academic readings and activities provide students with opportunities to draw upon life experience in their mastery of a wide variety of strategies and skills, including

- previewing
- scanning
- using context clues to clarify meaning
- finding the main idea
- summarizing
- making inferences.

Rich vocabulary instruction and practice that targets vocabulary from the Academic Word List (AWL) provide opportunities for students to improve their language proficiency and their ability to decode and process vocabulary.

A Closer Look at Academic Vocabulary

Academic vocabulary consists of those words which are used broadly in all academic domains, but are not necessarily frequent in other domains. They are words in the academic register that are needed by students who intend to pursue higher education. They are not the technical words used in one academic field or another (e.g., *genetics, fiduciary, proton*), but are found in all academic areas, often in a supportive role (*substitute, function, inhibit*).

The most principled and widely accepted list of academic words to date is The Academic Word List (AWL), compiled by Averil Coxhead in 2000. Its selection was based on a corpus of 3.5 million words of running text from academic materials across four academic disciplines: the humanities, business, law, and the physical and life sciences. The criteria for selection of the 570 word families on the AWL was that the words appear frequently and uniformly across a wide range of academic texts, and that they not appear among the first 2000 most common words of English, as identified by the General Service List.[6]

Across the four levels of *Inside Reading*, students are introduced to the 570 word families of the AWL at a gradual pace of about 15 words per unit. Their usage is authentic, the readings in which they appear are high interest, and the words are practiced and recycled in a variety of activities, facilitating both reading comprehension and word learning.

There has been a great deal of research into the optimal classroom conditions for facilitating word learning. This research points to several key factors.

Noticing: Before new words can be learned, they must be noticed. Schmidt, in his well-known *noticing hypothesis*, states

noticing is the necessary and sufficient condition for converting input into intake. Incidental learning, on the other hand, is clearly both possible and effective when the demands of a task focus attention on what is to be learned.[7]

Inside Reading facilitates noticing in two ways. Target words are printed in boldface type at their first occurrence to draw the students' attention to their context, usage, and word form. Students are then offered repeated opportunities to focus on them in activities and discussions. *Inside Reading* also devotes activities and tasks to particular target words. This is often accompanied by a presentation box giving information about the word, its family members, and its usage.

Teachers can further facilitate noticing by pre-teaching selected words through "rich instruction," meaning instruction that focuses on what it means to know a word, looks at the word in more than one setting, and involves learners in actively processing the word.[8] *Inside Reading* facilitates rich instruction by providing engaging activities that use and spotlight target words in both written and oral practice.

Repetition: Word learning is incremental. A learner is able to pick up new knowledge about a word with each encounter. Repetition also assists learner memory—multiple exposures at varying intervals dramatically enhance retention.

Repetition alone doesn't account for learning; the types and intervals of repetitions are also important.

---

6 West, 1953; Coxhead 2000
7 Schmidt, 1990, p. 129
8 Nation, 2001, p. 157

Research shows that words are best retained when the practice with a new word is brief but the word is repeated several times at increasing intervals.[9] *Inside Reading* provides multiple exposures to words at varying intervals and recycles vocabulary throughout the book to assist this process.

Learner involvement: Word-learning activities are not guaranteed to be effective simply by virtue of being interactive or communicative. Activities or tasks are most effective when learners are most *involved* in them. Optimal involvement is characterized by a learner's own perceived need for the unknown word, the desire to search for the information needed for the task, and the effort expended to compare the word to other words. It has been found that the greater the level of learner involvement, the better the retention.[10]

The activities in *Inside Reading* provide opportunities to be involved in the use of target words at two levels:

- "Word level," where words are practiced in isolation for the purpose of focusing on such aspects as meaning, derivation, grammatical features, and associations.
- "Sentence level," where learners respond to the readings by writing and paraphrasing sentences.

Because the activities are grounded in the two high-interest readings of each unit, they provide the teacher with frequent opportunities to optimize learner involvement.

Instruction and practice with varying types of word knowledge: To know a word means to know a great deal about the word.[11] The activities in this book include practice with all aspects of word knowledge: form (both oral and written), meaning, multiple meanings, collocations, grammatical features, derivatives, register, and associations.

Helping students become independent word learners: No single course or book can address all of the words a learner will need. Students should leave a class with new skills and strategies for word learning so that they can notice and effectively practice new words as they encounter them. *Inside Reading* includes several features to help guide students to becoming independent word learners. One is a self-assessment activity, which begins and ends each unit. Students evaluate their level of knowledge of each word, ranging from not knowing a word at all, to word recognition, and then to two levels of word use. This exercise demonstrates the incremental nature of word knowledge, and guides learners toward identifying what they know and what they need to know. Students can make better progress if they accurately identify the aspects of word knowledge they need for themselves. Another feature is the use of references and online resources: To further prepare students to be independent word learners, instruction and practice in dictionary use and online resources are provided throughout the book.

The *Inside Reading* Program

Inside Reading offers students and teachers helpful ancillaries:

Student CD-ROM: The CD-ROM in the back of every student book contains additional practice activities for students to work with on their own. The activities are self-correcting and allow students to redo an activity as many times as they wish.

Instructor's pack: The Instructor's pack contains the answer key for the book along with a test generator CD-ROM. The test generator contains one test per student book unit. Each test consists of a reading passage related to the topic of the unit, which features the target vocabulary. This is followed by reading comprehension and vocabulary questions. Teachers can use each unit's test in full or customize it in a variety of ways.

Inside Reading optimizes the reciprocal relationship between reading and vocabulary by drawing upon considerable research and many years of teaching experience. It provides the resources to help students read well and to use that knowledge to develop both a rich academic vocabulary and overall academic language proficiency.

---

[9] Research findings are inconclusive about the number of repetitions that are needed for retention. Estimates range from 6 to 20. See Nation, 2001, for a discussion of repetition and learning.

[10] Laufer & Hulstijn, 2001

[11] Nation, 1990; 2001

References

Carrel, P.L., Devine, J., & Eskey, D.E. (1988). *Interactive approaches to second language reading*. Cambridge: Cambridge University Press. (Or use "Holding in the bottom" by Eskey)

Coxhead, A. (2000). A new academic word list. *TESOL Quarterly, 34*, 213–238.

Eskey, D.E. (1988). Holding in the bottom. In P.L. Carrel, J. Devine, & D.E. Eskey, *Interactive approaches to second language reading*, pp. 93–100. Cambridge: Cambridge University Press.

Koda, K. (2005). *Insights into second language reading*. Cambridge: Cambridge University Press.

Laufer, B. (2005). Instructed second language vocabulary learning: The fault in the 'default hypothesis.' In A. Housen & M. Pierrard (Eds.), *Investigations in Instructed Second Language Acquisition*, pp. 286–303. New York: Mouton de Gruyter.

Laufer, B. (1992). Reading in a foreign language: How does L2 lexical knowledge interact with the reader's general academic ability? *Journal of Research in Reading, 15*(2), 95–103.

Nation, I.S.P. (1990). *Teaching and learning vocabulary*. New York: Newbury House.

Nation, I.S.P. (2001). *Learning vocabulary in another language*. Cambridge: Cambridge University Press.

Schmidt, R. (1990). The role of consciousness in second language learning. *Applied Linguistics, 11*, 129–158.

Schmitt, N. (2000). *Vocabulary in language teaching*. Cambridge: Cambridge University Press.

Schmitt, N. & Zimmerman, C.B. (2002). Derivative word forms: What do learners know? *TESOL Quarterly, 36*(2), 145–171.

Stahl, S.A. & Fairbanks, M.M. (1986). The effects of vocabulary instruction: A model-based meta-analysis. *Review of Educational Research, 56*(1), 72–110.

Welcome to *Inside Reading*

Inside Reading is a four-level series that develops students' abilities to interact with and access academic reading and vocabulary, preparing them for success in the academic classroom.

There are ten units in *Inside Reading*. Each unit features two readings on a high-interest topic from an academic content area, one or more reading skills and strategies, and work with a set of target word families from the **Academic Word List**.

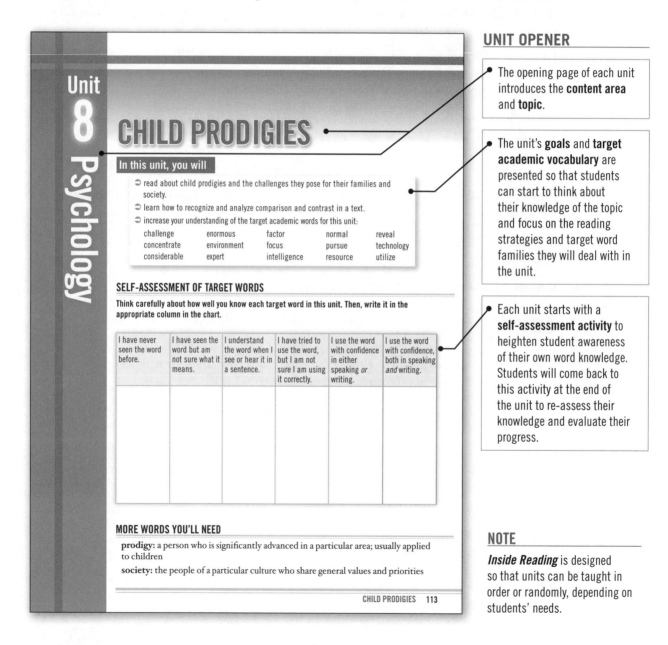

UNIT OPENER

- The opening page of each unit introduces the **content area** and **topic**.

- The unit's **goals** and **target academic vocabulary** are presented so that students can start to think about their knowledge of the topic and focus on the reading strategies and target word families they will deal with in the unit.

- Each unit starts with a **self-assessment activity** to heighten student awareness of their own word knowledge. Students will come back to this activity at the end of the unit to re-assess their knowledge and evaluate their progress.

Unit 8 — Psychology

CHILD PRODIGIES

In this unit, you will

- read about child prodigies and the challenges they pose for their families and society.
- learn how to recognize and analyze comparison and contrast in a text.
- increase your understanding of the target academic words for this unit:

challenge	enormous	factor	normal	reveal
concentrate	environment	focus	pursue	technology
considerable	expert	intelligence	resource	utilize

SELF-ASSESSMENT OF TARGET WORDS

Think carefully about how well you know each target word in this unit. Then, write it in the appropriate column in the chart.

I have never seen the word before.	I have seen the word but am not sure what it means.	I understand the word when I see or hear it in a sentence.	I have tried to use the word, but I am not sure I am using it correctly.	I use the word with confidence in either speaking *or* writing.	I use the word with confidence, both in speaking *and* writing.

MORE WORDS YOU'LL NEED

prodigy: a person who is significantly advanced in a particular area; usually applied to children

society: the people of a particular culture who share general values and priorities

CHILD PRODIGIES   113

NOTE

Inside Reading is designed so that units can be taught in order or randomly, depending on students' needs.

READING 1

BEFORE YOU READ

Read these questions. Discuss your answers in a small group.

1. Have you ever known anyone who was very, very smart? What could they do or what did they know that made them different from other people their age?

2. What can a family do to help or encourage a baby's mental development? Physical development? Emotional development?

3. Schools often want to know how intelligent children are. How do schools usually measure intelligence? What kinds of tools or tests do they use? What skills or abilities do they measure?

READ

This magazine article spotlights the unusual abilities of some very special children.

Child Prodigies

It seemed **normal** when Nguyen Ngoc Truong Son wanted to play chess with his parents. However, it was unusual when he **revealed** that he already knew how to play—before anyone
5 taught him. Apparently the two-year-old had learned all of the rules by watching his parents. After only one month of playing with them, he was winning all of the games. By age 4, he was competing in national tournaments. By age 12,
10 he was Vietnam's youngest champion.

Another two-year-old child, Jay Greenberg, likewise surprised his parents by drawing pictures of musical instruments that he had never seen. They soon discovered that Jay
15 "heard music in his head." He began to compose music at age 3. By age 10, he was attending the prestigious Julliard Conservatory in New York, composing full symphonies. Jay was noted not only for the quality of his musical work, but also
20 the speed at which he was able to produce it. That is, while talented professional composers normally write five or six symphonies in a lifetime, Jay wrote five by the age of 12.

A third young child, Abigail Sin, was first
25 introduced to piano lessons at age 5 and had what her tutor called an "unstoppable urge to master the keyboard." She became Singapore's most celebrated pianist by age 10.

30 Child prodigies such as these are a mystery to **experts** and non-experts alike. On the one hand, they attract praise and attention from everyone they meet; on the other hand, they attract criticism and they find it difficult to fit in with the rest of the world.

35 Child prodigies are highly intelligent, but this is not the only **factor** that sets them apart. They are considered prodigies because of their exceptional ability in one domain, or area. Experts define *prodigy* as "a young child
40 who displays mastery of a field that is usually undertaken by adults." Child prodigies usually appear in structured areas such as language, math, drawing, chess, and music. They are not as likely to appear in less structured domains
45 such as medicine, law, or creative writing, areas that require experience.

114   UNIT 8

READING COMPREHENSION

READING COMPREHENSION

Mark each sentence as *T* (true) or *F* (false) according to the information in Reading 1. Use the dictionary to help you understand new words.

.... 1. The parents of two-year-old Nguyen Ngoc Truong Son taught him to play chess and he learned very quickly.

.... 2. The parents of Jay Greenberg did not provide an environment that was focused on music, but young Jay had great interest in music at a very young age.

.... 3. Jay Greenberg wrote symphonies very quickly because he utilized the help of talented professional composers.

.... 4. The factors that seem to always be present in a child prodigy are 1) an unusually high intelligence and 2) the ability to master one area, such as music or math.

.... The child prodigies mentioned in the reading showed considerable interest

---

Before each of the two readings in a unit, students discuss questions to activate knowledge of the specific topic dealt with in the reading.

Readings represent a variety of genres: newspapers, magazines, web sites, press releases, encyclopedias, and books.

Target vocabulary is bold at its first occurrence to aid recognition. Vocabulary is recycled and practiced throughout the unit. Target words are also recycled in subsequent units.

Reading comprehension questions follow each text to check students' understanding and recycle target vocabulary.

READING STRATEGIES

Strategy presentation and **practice** accompanies each reading.

READING STRATEGY: Recognizing Comparison and Contrast

Writers often compare things and ideas to show how they are similar. They also contrast things and ideas to show how they are different. Comparisons and contrasts are important in helping the reader understand how things and ideas relate to each other. You can recognize comparisons and contrasts by the context clues that signal them.

A. Read these context clues. Write *S* for those that indicate similarity (comparison) or *D* for those that indicate difference (contrast). Compare your answers with a partner.

_S_ both	_____ in the same way	_____ on the contrary
_____ but	_____ instead of	_____ on the other hand
_____ despite	_____ likewise	_____ similarly
_____ however	_____ moreover	_____ unlike

VOCABULARY ACTIVITIES

The vocabulary work following each reading **starts at word level**. Step I activities are mostly receptive and focus on meanings and word family members.

STEP I VOCABULARY ACTIVITIES: Word Level

A. Read these excerpts from another article on child prodigies. For each excerpt, cross out the one word or phrase in parentheses with a different meaning from the other three choices. Compare your answers with a partner.

1. Parents can create a positive or a negative environment for their highly intelligent children. The mother of 6-year-old Hungarian cellist Janos Starker wanted her son to (*display / concentrate on / focus on / think about*) his music practice, so she made tiny sandwiches and left them on his music stand. She didn't want him to have to get up and look for a snack.

2. Given the results, we should not be critical of this mother's methods. Janos Starker's (*considerable / great / expert / extensive*) success as an international cellist lasted over 50 years and his is one of the great musical careers of our time.

3. Another musician to (*reveal / display / utilize / demonstrate*) exceptional musical promise was pianist Ruth Slezynska. She performed at a major concert for the first time in 1929 at the age of four.

4. Whereas Starker's mother encouraged him with tiny sandwiches, Slezynska's father created (*a feeling / an environment / an atmosphere / a setting*) of fear. He forced her to practice nine hours every day and hit her when she played a wrong note.

Vocabulary work then **progresses to the sentence level**. Step II activities are mostly productive and feature work with collocations and specific word usage. These activities can also include work with register, associations, connotations, and learner dictionaries.

STEP II VOCABULARY ACTIVITIES: Sentence Level

Word Form Chart			
Noun	Verb	Adjective	Adverb
challenge	challenge	challenging challenged*	....

E. Answer the questions using each form of *challenge* at least once. Refer to Reading 1 for information. Discuss your answers in a small group or as a class.

1. How did the Greenbergs feel about raising Jay?

   For the Greenbergs, raising a child prodigy was a challenge, but they enjoyed supporting him and encouraging his interests.

2. What were some of the difficulties faced by Billy Sidis in his adult life?

   ....

   ....

3. What difficulties do researchers or experts face as they try to better understand child prodigies?

   ....

   ....

4. What difficulties do child prodigies pose for society?

   ....

   ....

NOTE

Each unit ends with topics and projects that teachers can use to take the lesson further. This section includes class discussion topics, online research projects, and essay ideas.

THE BIRTH OF THE MALL

In this unit, you will

- ➲ read about the origin of the modern shopping mall and the refugee architect who created it.
- ➲ learn to preview a reading text in order to predict what it will be about.
- ➲ increase your understanding of the target academic words for this unit:

academy	construct	function	publication	select
approach	couple	partner	range	simulate
concept	enhance	pose	region	uniform

SELF-ASSESSMENT OF TARGET WORDS

Learning a word is a gradual process.

- First, you learn to *recognize* the word. This means you know something about its spelling, pronunciation, and meanings.
- Next, you learn to *use* the word. This requires that you understand its spelling, pronunciation, grammar, and much more.

When you truly know a word, you can both recognize it and use it accurately.

Read the target words for this unit in the objectives box above. Think carefully about how well you know each word. Then, write each word in the appropriate column in this chart.

I have never seen the word before.	I have seen the word but am not sure what it means.	I understand the word when I see or hear it in a sentence.	I have tried to use the word, but I am not sure I am using it correctly.	I use the word with confidence in either speaking *or* writing.	I use the word with confidence, both in speaking *and* writing.

BEFORE YOU READ

Read these questions. Discuss your answers in a small group.

1. Where is your closest indoor shopping mall? How often do you go there? What types of things do you usually buy there? What types of things can you NOT find there?

2. Besides shopping, what else is there to do at the mall? Are there things just for people your age? For young children? For older people?

3. Do you think that shopping malls are part of a community or something separate from it? Why?

READING STRATEGY: Previewing and Predicting

Previewing a text helps you predict what the text is going to be about. This helps prepare you for taking in information and remembering it.

Before reading a text, preview it:

- Read the titles or headlines.
- Look at the pictures and read the captions.
- Skim the text for commonly mentioned names and details.

This allows you to *anticipate the topic* of the text and get your mind ready to learn more about it.

A. Skim Reading 1. Look for and note these things.

1. A frequently named person: ....

2. A frequently mentioned building: ....

3. Some dates: ....

4. Some locations: ....

B. Make some predictions about Reading 1. After you've read the text, come back to check your predictions.

1. Who is the most important person in the reading? ....

2. About when did the events take place? ....

3. Where did some of the events take place? ....

4. What is this text going to be about? ....

....

This magazine feature article traces the history of the first indoor shopping mall and its designer.

The Terrazzo[1] Jungle

Shopping malls are symbols of suburban life in the United States. The idea for this most American of architectural landmarks, however, came from a European immigrant, Victor Gruen.

5 Victor Gruen grew up in Vienna, Austria, studying architecture at the Vienna **Academy** of Fine Arts, the same school that had previously turned down a fledgling artist named Adolf Hitler. At night, Gruen performed theater in 10 smoke-filled cafes around the city. When Hitler's Nazis invaded Austria in 1938, Gruen decided to emigrate. One of his theater friends—**posing** as an officer in a Nazi **uniform**—drove Gruen and his wife to the airport. They took the first plane 15 they could catch to Zurich, Switzerland, made their way to England, and then obtained passage on a ship bound for New York. They landed in the United States, as Gruen later remembered, "with an architect's degree, eight dollars, and no 20 English."

One day, Gruen went for a walk in midtown Manhattan and ran into an old friend from Vienna who wanted to open a leather-goods boutique on Fifth Avenue. Gruen agreed to design it, and 25 the result was a revolutionary storefront, with a kind of mini-arcade in the entranceway: six exquisite glass cases, spotlights, and faux[2] marble, with green corrugated glass on the ceiling. It was a "customer trap." This was a brand-new idea 30 in American retail design, particularly on Fifth Avenue, where all the storefronts were facing the street. The critics raved[3].

Gruen designed Ciro's on Fifth Avenue, Steckler's on Broadway, Paris Decorators on the 35 Bronx Concourse, and eleven branches of the California clothing chain Grayson's. In the early 1950s, he designed an outdoor shopping center called Northland, outside Detroit, Michigan. It

An example of "customer trap" design

covered one hundred and sixty-three acres and 40 had nearly ten thousand parking spaces. This was little more than a decade and a half since he had stepped off the boat. When Gruen watched the bulldozers break ground, he turned to his **partner** and said, "We've got a lot of nerve."

45 Gruen's most famous creation was his next project, in the town of Edina, just outside Minneapolis, Minnesota. It was called Southdale Mall. Until then, most shopping centers had been what architects like to call "extroverted," 50 meaning that store windows and entrances faced both the parking area and the interior pedestrian walkways. Southdale was "introverted"—the exterior walls were blank, and all the activity was focused on the inside. Suburban shopping 55 centers had always been in the open, with stores connected by outdoor passageways. Gruen had the radical idea of putting the whole complex under one roof, with air-conditioning in the summer and heating in the winter.

60 Work on Southdale began in 1954. It cost twenty million dollars and took two years to **construct**. It had seventy-two stores and two anchor department stores, Donaldson's on one end and Dayton's on the other.

---

[1] *terrazzo*: a flooring material made of marble and used indoors, often in large public spaces
[2] *faux*: imitation
[3] *rave*: praise something highly

Southdale, completed in 1956, was the first modern shopping mall.

65   Almost every other major shopping center was on a single level, which made for long walks. Gruen's **approach** was to put stores on two levels, connected by escalators and fed by two-tiered parking. In the middle, he put a kind of
70 town square: a "garden court" under a skylight, with a fishpond, enormous sculpted trees, a twenty-one-foot cage filled with brightly colored birds, balconies with hanging plants, and a cafe.

    The result was a sensation. Journalists from
75 all of the country's top **publications** came for Southdale's opening. "The Splashiest Center in the U. S.," wrote one magazine. "A pleasure dome with parking," cheered another. One journalist announced that overnight Southdale
80 had become an integral "part of the American Way." It **simulated** a magnetic urban downtown area in the middle of suburbia: the variety, the individuality, the lights, the color, and the crowds. This downtown essence was **enhanced**
85 by all kinds of things that ought to be there if downtown areas weren't so noisy and dirty and chaotic, such as sidewalk cafes, art, islands of planting, and pretty paving. Other shopping centers, however pleasant, seemed provincial[4]

90 in contrast with the real thing, the city's downtown. In Minneapolis, however, it was the downtown that appeared small and provincial in contrast to Southdale's metropolitan character.

    One person who wasn't dazzled by Gruen's
95 **concept** was the famous architect Frank Lloyd Wright. "What is this, a railroad station or a bus station?" he asked, when he came for a tour of Southdale. "You've got a garden court that has all the evils of the village street and none of its
100 charm." No one listened to Frank Lloyd Wright. When it came to malls, it was only Victor Gruen's vision that mattered.

    Southdale Mall still exists—a big concrete box in a sea of parking. The anchor tenants
105 are now J. C. Penney and Marshall Field's, and there is just about every other chain store that you've ever seen in a mall. It does not seem like a historic building, which is precisely why it is one. Fifty years ago, Victor Gruen designed a
110 fully enclosed, introverted, multitiered, double-anchor shopping complex with a garden court under a skylight. Today, virtually every **regional** shopping center in America is a fully enclosed, introverted, multitiered, double-anchor complex
115 with a garden court under a skylight.

    Victor Gruen didn't design a building; he designed an archetype[5]. Over the past half century that archetype—for what Gruen himself has called "a gigantic shopping machine"—has
120 been reproduced so faithfully so many thousands of times that today nearly every suburban resident goes shopping or wanders around or hangs out in a Southdale facsimile at least once or twice a month. Victor Gruen may well
125 have been the most influential architect of the twentieth century. He invented the mall.

---

[4] *provincial*: unsophisticated
[5] *archetype*: the original model for something, which all others copy

READING COMPREHENSION

Mark each sentence as *T* (true) or *F* (false) according to the information in Reading 1. Use your dictionary to check new words.

.... **1.** Victor Gruen started working as an architect as soon as he arrived in New York.

.... **2.** Gruen is also known for designing storefronts that functioned as "customer traps."

.... **3.** Southdale was the first regional shopping center in the United States.

.... **4.** Southdale is an enclosed mall, with very few windows looking outside.

.... **5.** When it opened, Southdale was widely praised by many publications and the public.

.... **6.** The well-known architect Frank Lloyd Wright considered Southdale to be a charming model for the future.

.... **7.** Southdale has been torn down because the Mall of America was constructed nearby.

.... **8.** Many shopping malls today have been designed to follow the Southdale form.

STEP I VOCABULARY ACTIVITIES: Word Level

A *partner* is someone associated with another person in some way and for some purpose. There are many types of *partners*. Some partnerships are related to work and business, while others function on a more personal level. These can relate to school, family life, politics, or even crime.

A. Look up these words in your dictionary. What type of partnership does each one suggest? There may be more than one answer for some words. Compare answers with a partner. Can you think of any other types of partnerships?

1. accomplice: *crime*

2. ally:

3. associate:

4. collaborator:

5. colleague:

Others:

6. co-worker:

7. roommate:

8. sidekick:

9. spouse:

10. teammate:

Word Form Chart

Noun	Verb	Adjective	Adverb
pose	pose	posed	....
uniform	....	uniform	uniformly
construction	construct	constructive	constructively
simulation	simulate	simulated	....
enhancement	enhance	enhanced	....
region	....	regional	regionally
concept	conceptualize	conceptual	conceptually

B. Using the target words in the chart, complete the sentences. Be sure to use the correct form and tense of each word.

1. One of Gruen's theater friends .... as a Nazi officer. He dressed
   (pretended to be)
   in a .... and drove Gruen and his wife to the airport.
   (military outfit)

2. Southdale was the first enclosed .... shopping center in the U.S.
   (area-wide)

3. The mall design attempts to .... the feeling of a downtown
   (imitate)
   urban area.

4. The social atmosphere of the mall was .... by including natural
   (improved)
   light and many plants.

5. Two years after Gruen proposed the .... , the
   (idea)
   .... of Southdale was completed.
   (building)

C. Work with a partner. Write down at least one example of each type of region.

1. a geographic region: *the Middle East* ....
2. a metropolitan region: ....
3. an industrial region: ....
4. an agricultural region: ....
5. a region known for a specific feature or activity: ....

STEP II VOCABULARY ACTIVITIES: Sentence Level

> The word *academy* generally refers to a school for special instruction or training, as in an art academy, military academy, or tennis academy.
>
> The adjective form, *academic*, refers to higher education in general—for example, this book focuses on the Academic Word List.

D. How important are these concepts for you as a student? Why? Write a complete sentence for each. Consult your dictionary, if needed. Be prepared to discuss your ideas with your classmates.

1. academic integrity ....
....

2. academic freedom ....
....

3. academic standards ....
....

4. academic community ....
....

E. Answer the questions using each form of *concept* at least once in your answers. Compare your sentences with a partner. Refer to Reading 1 for information.

1. How was Gruen's shopping mall different from other regional shopping centers of that time?
2. How did Gruen's experience with theater enhance his architectural work?
3. If Gruen had stayed in Europe or emigrated to a different country, do you think he would have invented the mall there? Why or why not?
4. Is shopping at a mall different from shopping in a typical downtown environment? Why or why not?
5. What are some factors that are fundamental to the design of a shopping mall? Why are they important?

The word *pose* has two verb forms. The first form is *intransitive*—it does not take an object. It means either "to sit for a portrait" or "to pretend to be other than what one is."

*Sometimes people don't like to **pose** for photos.*

*Gruen's theater friend **posed** as a Nazi officer.*

The second form is *transitive*—it must have an object. It means "to present, raise, put forward, bring up, or propose something."

*The climate in Minnesota—very cold in the winter, rainy and hot in the summer— **posed** <u>a challenge</u> to Victor Gruen as he began the Southdale project.*

F. Think of things that pose questions or concerns for you, your region, or for the planet in general. Write complete sentences and be prepared to explain your ideas to your classmates.

1. Something that poses a concern

For you: ....

For your region: ....

For our planet: ....

2. Something that poses an opportunity

For you: ....

For your region: ....

For our planet: ....

3. Something that poses a challenge

For you: ....

For your region: ....

For our planet: ....

4. Something that poses a threat

For you: ....

For your region: ....

For our planet: ....

5. Something that poses a difficult choice, or *dilemma*

For you: ....

For your region: ....

For our planet: ....

BEFORE YOU READ

Read these questions. Discuss your answers in a small group.

1. What is the function of a press release? Who is the audience?

2. What information do you think should be in a press release? What information should not be in it?

3. Think about the first reading in this unit. Do you think the publicity for Southdale Mall was successful? Why or why not? How do you know?

READING STRATEGY

As you preview a text for the general topic, you should also think about the *focus* of it.

First, preview the reading:

- Read the titles or headlines.
- Look at the pictures and read the captions.
- Skim the text for commonly mentioned names and details.

Then, ask yourself these questions:

- How is the reading organized?
- Who is the audience?
- What is the writer trying to accomplish?

Understanding the focus of the text will help you understand the writer's purpose for it.

Preview Reading 2 and answer these questions. After you've read the text, come back to check your answers.

1. What is the text about? ....

2. Who wrote this text? ....

3. What is the purpose of the text? ....

4. How does the focus differ from Reading 1? ....

....

This press release was one of several announcing the opening of the Southdale Mall. It is typical of press releases for many different types of projects.

FOR RELEASE: October 7, 1956
FROM: Harry Levine
Ruder & Finn, Incorporated
130 East 59 Street
New York, 22, New York
Plaza 9-1800
FOR: DAYTON'S SOUTHDALE CENTER
THE ARCHITECTS OF SOUTHDALE
I. VICTOR GRUEN & ASSOCIATES

Victor Gruen & Associates is a planning team of architects and engineers with headquarters in Los Angeles and offices in Detroit, New York, Minneapolis, and San Francisco.

5   Actively engaged in projects in almost every state as well as abroad, the Gruen organization was chosen as architect for Southdale in 1952.

The five partners of the firm, Victor Gruen, Karl Van Leuven, Jr., R. L. Baumfeld, Edgardo
10 Contini, and Ben S. Southland, were brought together in the common belief that individual ingenuity **coupled** with disciplined teamwork offers the best approach to today's complex problems in planning.

15 As senior partner, Victor Gruen is responsible for the concept development of major projects. R. L. Baumfeld heads the Los Angeles office and has been in charge of many large projects, among them the Southdale Center. Edgardo Contini
20 directs engineering for the firm and is in charge of coordinating engineering and architectural design. Karl Van Leuven, Jr., head of the Detroit office, has been partner in charge of such major projects as Northland Regional Shopping Center
25 in Detroit. Ben S. Southland is chief designer and director of planning.

Herman Guttman, project coordinator for the Southdale Shopping Center, is head of the Victor Gruen Minneapolis office and an associate in
30 the firm.

Victor Gruen & Associates has steadily expanded the **range** of its activities. In the commercial field, the firm has progressed from the planning of individual shops and department
35 stores to the development of planned regional shopping centers that have changed American shopping habits.

In the residential field, Victor Gruen & Associates has planned everything from
40 individual houses, apartments, and housing projects to complete community developments that meet all the needs of modern living.

Among Gruen projects of special interest are:

Milliron's Department Store (now The
45 Broadway) in Los Angeles, the first one-story department store with roof parking.

The Mid-Wilshire Medical Building and two 13-story Tishman Buildings in Los Angeles, all representing advances in design and planning
50 (lightweight steel buildings).

A number of large regional shopping centers throughout the country, among them Northland in Detroit, the world's largest. Others include Eastland, also in suburban Detroit, Glendale
55 in Indianapolis, Valley Fair and Bay Fair, both in the San Francisco Bay area, and South Bay in Redondo Beach, California. (The latter in association with Quincy Jones and Frederick Emmons, Architects A.I.A.).

60 Master planning for the Palos Verdes Peninsula, providing for residential, civic, commercial, educational, and recreational development of an outstanding land area of 7000 acres.

65 Master planning for the redevelopment of a downtown area in Detroit (the Gratiot-Orleans

area), in association with Oskar Stonorov and Minoru Yamasaki.

A comprehensive study for redevelopment of the entire downtown area of Fort Worth, Texas. The study has produced a dramatic plan for renewal of the heart of the city through a long-range program aimed at solving traffic, parking, and urban rehabilitation problems.

The Gruen organization created the master plan for Southdale, in addition to designing the regional shopping center. In addition to Dayton's, it designed the following stores and special facilities:

Egekvist Bakery, Boutell's, Walters, the First National Bank, Thorpe Bros., J. B. Hudson Company, Juster Bros., Peter Pan Restaurant, Bringgold Meat Company, Bjorkman's, Edina Liquor Store, Sidewalk Café, Garner Records, The Children's Center, and The Toy Fair.

II. VICTOR GRUEN

Victor Gruen, the head of Victor Gruen & Associates, was born in Vienna, Austria, where he received his architectural training at the Technological Institute, Advanced Division for Building Construction, and the Academy of Fine Arts. He was certified as an architect in Vienna in 1929 and practiced in that city until 1938, when he moved to the United States and opened his first office in New York. He is a registered architect in many states and his firm now has offices in Los Angeles, Detroit, New York, Minneapolis, and San Francisco.

Gruen's early work was in the fields of individual store design and residential projects. He is regarded as a pioneer in modern store design in work ranging from small shops to large department stores. Gruen turned to shopping center design early as a challenging new field of architectural expression. He again won praise. As this firm expanded, the scope of his professional work grew to include such diverse projects as office buildings, private homes, public and tract housing projects, and the planning of complete communities including homes, apartment buildings, office buildings, shopping centers, civic buildings, schools, and recreational facilities. His unique achievements in these fields, especially in the design of shopping centers, have led him in recent years into the field of city planning and urban redevelopment.

Gruen's work has been widely published in such professional publications as PROGRESSIVE ARCHITECTURE and ARCHITECTURAL FORUM; in professional books such as SHOPS AND STORES and FORMS AND **FUNCTIONS** OF TWENTIETH CENTURY ARCHITECTURE; in technical and trade publications such as LIGHTING, ENGINEERING NEWS RECORD, THE AMERICAN CITY, and in FORTUNE, BUSINESS WEEK, THE SATURDAY EVENING POST, LIFE, THE NEW YORKER, COLLIER'S, LADIES HOME JOURNAL, McCALL'S, and HARVARD BUSINESS REVIEW.

He has spoken frequently before professional, technical, business, and planning groups and has written many articles for professional, trade, and business publications, and is presently working on two books. He has been **selected** for numerous awards for outstanding architectural work by the American Institute of Architects and other groups.

Of special interest is Gruen's comprehensive study of shopping center planning, written in collaboration with Lawrence P. Smith, which comprised the entire June 1952 issue of PROGRESSIVE ARCHITECTURE; and a traveling exhibition, "The Shopping Center of Tomorrow," created for the American Federation of Arts and shown in leading museums throughout the United States and abroad.

READING COMPREHENSION

Mark each sentence as *T* (true) or *F* (false) according to the information in Reading 2.

.... **1.** Victor Gruen's firm consists only of architects.

.... **2.** The firm has designed both commercial and residential projects.

.... **3.** As senior partner, Gruen is mainly responsible for developing project concepts.

.... **4.** When they began construction on Southdale, Gruen and his partners had little experience designing shopping centers.

.... **5.** Gruen and his partners designed not only the shopping center but also several of the stores and facilities inside the center.

.... **6.** This firm has offices in several cities.

.... **7.** Gruen's work is of little interest to other professional architects.

.... **8.** According to the press release, the development of planned regional shopping centers has changed American shopping habits.

STEP I VOCABULARY ACTIVITIES: Word Level

A. Complete the sentences about Victor Gruen using the target vocabulary in the box. Use each item one time. The synonyms in parentheses can help you.

approach to	enhanced	select
concept	functions	simulate
construct	posed	
couple	range	

1. In his .... designing Southdale, Victor Gruen
   (way of thinking about)
   .... several important questions.
   (raised)

2. How could a shopping center be .... and made more
   (improved)
   comfortable in all kinds of weather?

3. Why would customers .... a shopping center that might be far
   (choose)
   from home?

4. In developing his basic .... Gruen also wondered what would
   (idea)
   cause customers to stay longer in the mall and buy more things.

5. He decided that it was important to .... the energy of the city
   (combine)
   with the order and cleanliness of the suburbs.

6. Gruen attempted to .... a big-city feeling in a small-town
(imitate)
   shopping center.

> The word _uniform_, as a noun, refers to the set of clothes worn by people in the same
> job or organization, for example, a military uniform or a football uniform.
>
> As an adjective, _uniform_ means "the same in all cases and at all times." It is often used
> for technical descriptions, for example, uniform standards for construction projects.

B. Which aspects of these things or situations should be uniform? Discuss your answers in a small group. What else should be uniform or have uniform aspects?

1. a busy city street
2. chain restaurants
3. textbooks used in one school
4. schools in different regions
5. workers in the same company
6. cars
7. other: ....
8. other: ....

C. Match the different types of publications with their descriptions. Use a dictionary if necessary.

.... 1. book

.... 2. magazine

.... 3. journal

.... 4. newspaper

.... 5. brochure

.... 6. booklet

.... 7. catalog

a. a thin glossy pamphlet with pictures in it that gives information about a specific product or program

b. a large-sized daily (or weekly) publication focusing on current events

c. a hard-cover or paperback publication containing a continuous story or narrative

d. a small publication that usually goes with another item, for example, instructions for using a product

e. a soft-cover publication focusing on a specific area of interest, for example, fashion, cars, or a sport

f. a soft-cover publication listing a store's products or a school's courses

g. a soft-cover publication sponsored by an academic or professional society and focused on issues in that field

D. Use the names of the publications in activity C (in the correct form) to complete the sentences.

1. At the student center, you can pick up a .... about study-abroad programs.

2. Most research libraries keep a range of .... from different organizations. When you need to find an academic or scientific article, you should check those first.

3. Some people don't like to go to the mall. They might prefer to order the things they want from a store's .... and have them sent to their home.

4. I want to read the new Harry Potter .... , but the hard-cover version is so expensive. I'll wait until it comes out in paperback in a couple of months.

5. Most video games come with an instruction .... that explains how to play the game.

6. My father reads the .... every morning because he wants to know what's happening in the world quickly. I prefer to read a weekly news .... because it has enhanced coverage of current events along with some analysis.

STEP II VOCABULARY ACTIVITIES: Sentence Level

The context of a sentence can help you learn how to use a word correctly. For this reason, dictionaries often include sample sentences that give you clues about meaning, collocations (words that go together), and levels of formality.

E. Read the sample sentences in the box that feature the words *approach* and *range*. Then, write a new sample sentence for each one, using *approach* or *range* in the same meaning and word form.

1. *Summer is approaching.*
2. *The truck approached the bridge.*
3. *Her performance approached perfection.*
4. *She approached her boss for a raise.*
5. *She used a logical approach to solve the problem.*
6. *Some cars are out of his price range.*
7. *His singing voice has a broad range.*
8. *The students ranged in age from fifteen to twenty-five.*
9. *The buffalo once ranged across western North America.*
10. *Computer manufacturers offer a wide range of product choices.*

1. *I have to buy him a present soon because his birthday is approaching.*
2. ....
3. ....
4. ....
5. ....
6. ....
7. ....
8. ....
9. ....
10. ....

F. Think about a traditional approach to these problems or situations. Summarize that approach briefly. Then, in a small group, imagine how a person in the academic field indicated might approach the same problem or situation, and summarize that approach.

1. Carrying a lot of books and notebooks to different classes
   Traditional: ....
   Engineer: ....
2. Staying dry while walking in the rain
   Traditional: ....
   Chemist: ....
3. Going to school and working full time
   Traditional: ....
   Computer scientist: ....
4. Selling a new line of kites
   Traditional: ....
   Meteorologist: ....
5. Serving lunch to 100 schoolchildren in half an hour
   Traditional: ....
   Architect: ....
6. Increasing the number of people who vote in elections
   Traditional: ....
   Marketing person: ....

Choose one of the problems in F and write a paragraph describing the new approach. Use your imagination. Be prepared to present your ideas to the class.

G. Self-Assessment Review: Go back to page 1 and reassess your knowledge of the target vocabulary. How has your understanding of the words changed? What words do you feel most comfortable with now?

WRITING AND DISCUSSION TOPICS

1. Describe your favorite shopping mall. Where is it? What is special about it? Which of Victor Gruen's Southdale features are also a part of your favorite mall?

2. Victor Gruen once described his creation as "a gigantic shopping machine." What do you think he meant?

3. How do you expect malls to change in the future? How would you enhance the mall of today to create the mall of the future?

4. What are the negative aspects of shopping malls and of shopping in malls? How are these negative aspects addressed in other shopping formats?

5. In addition to shopping malls, what are some other environments where people do their shopping? For example, where/how do people living in a rural setting shop for things they need? Or, where might people living in a big city—like New York, Beijing, or Sao Paulo—do their shopping?

6. According to the 1956 press release (Reading 2), the development of planned regional shopping centers changed the traditional approach to shopping and traditional concepts of shopping. Do you think the Internet will have as big an impact on shopping habits as malls did? Why or why not?

MEGACITIES

In this unit, you will

⇀ read about the development of modern cities and regional megacities—and what the future holds for urban life around the globe.

⇀ practice identifying and outlining main ideas in a reading selection.

⇀ increase your understanding of the target academic words for this unit:

communicate	extract	migrate	rely	status
define	globe	network	remove	survive
despite	major	perspective	source	

SELF-ASSESSMENT OF TARGET WORDS

Think carefully about how well you know each target word in this unit. Then, write it in the appropriate column in the chart.

I have never seen the word before.	I have seen the word but am not sure what it means.	I understand the word when I see or hear it in a sentence.	I have tried to use the word, but I am not sure I am using it correctly.	I use the word with confidence in either speaking *or* writing.	I use the word with confidence, both in speaking *and* writing.

MORE WORDS YOU'LL NEED

megalopolis: an urban region, especially one consisting of several large cities and suburbs that are all connected to each other (from the Greek "mega," meaning *large*, and "polis," meaning *city*)

ecopolis: a city considered in relationship to its environment (from the Greek "eco," meaning *house*, or more broadly *surroundings*, and "polis," meaning *city*)

BEFORE YOU READ

Read these questions. Discuss your answers in a small group.

1. What is the biggest city you've ever visited? What did you like about it? Was there anything you didn't like? Why or why not?

2. How big is your city—in geographic size and in population? Would you say your city is small, medium-sized, large, or extremely large? Why?

3. Think about the cities near where you live. How near are other major cities? Are there any smaller suburban communities surrounding your city? What reasons or factors can you think of to explain the pattern of urban development in your area?

READ

This article from *Newsweek* magazine is about the rise of megacities.

The New Megalopolis

Our focus on cities is wrong. Growth and innovation come from new urban corridors.

China isn't the world's most ferocious new economic competitor—the exploding east-coast corridor, from Beijing to Shanghai, is. India as a whole is not developing high-
5 tech industries and attracting jobs, but the booming mega-region stretching from Bangalore to Hyderabad is. Across the world, in fact, nations don't spur growth so much as dynamic regions—modern versions of the
10 original "megalopolis," a term coined by the geographer Jean Gottman to identify the sprawling Boston–New York–Washington economic power corridor.

The New Megas are the real economic
15 organizing units of the world and the **major sources** of **global** wealth, attracting a large share of its talent and generating the most innovation. They take shape as powerful complexes of multiple cities and suburbs,
20 often stretching across national borders—forming a vast expanse of trade, transport, **communications**, and talent. Yet, **despite** the fact that the rise of regions has been apparent for more than a decade, no one has collected
25 systematic information on them—not the World Bank, not the IMF[1], not the United Nations, not the global consulting firms.

That's why a team of geographers set about building a world map of the New Megas
30 shaped by satellite images of the world at night, using light emissions to **define** the outlines of each region, and additional data in categories such as population and economic growth to chart their relative peak
35 strengths and dynamism[2]. The result is the topographical map you see here.

The map makes it clear that the global economy takes shape around perhaps 20 great Megas—half in the United States and the
40 rest scattered throughout the world. These regions are home to just 10 percent of total world population, 660 million people, but produce half of all economic activity, two thirds of world-class scientific activity, and
45 three quarters of global innovations. The great urbanologist Jane Jacobs was the first to describe why megalopolises grow. When people **migrate** to one place, they all become

---

[1] *IMF*: International Monetary Fund, a financial monitoring and regulating organization
[2] *dynamism*: the pattern or process of change, growth, and activity

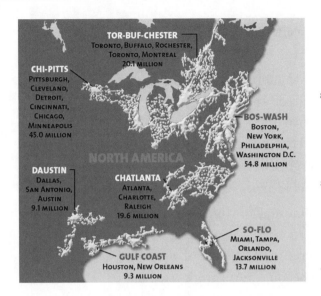

TOR-BUF-CHESTER
TORONTO, BUFFALO, ROCHESTER,
TORONTO, MONTREAL
20.1 MILLION

CHI-PITTS
PITTSBURGH,
CLEVELAND,
DETROIT,
CINCINNATI,
CHICAGO,
MINNEAPOLIS
45.0 MILLION

BOS-WASH
BOSTON,
NEW YORK,
PHILADELPHIA,
WASHINGTON D.C.
54.8 MILLION

NORTH AMERICA

DAUSTIN
DALLAS,
SAN ANTONIO,
AUSTIN
9.1 MILLION

CHATLANTA
ATLANTA,
CHARLOTTE,
RALEIGH
19.6 MILLION

SO-FLO
MIAMI, TAMPA,
ORLANDO,
JACKSONVILLE
13.7 MILLION

GULF COAST
HOUSTON, NEW ORLEANS
9.3 MILLION

more productive. And the place itself becomes
50 much more productive, because collective
creativity grows exponentially[3]. Ideas flow
more freely, are honed[4] more sharply, and can
be put into practice more quickly.

There is, however, a tipping point[5]. The
55 forces of price and congestion begin pushing
people away from the center. But make no
mistake, this has nothing to do with the
"decentralization of work," as many have
argued. The huge economic advantages of
60 clustering still guide the process, which is why
second cities emerge near big cities or in the
corridors between them, not in the middle of
nowhere.

The first region to achieve Mega **status** and
65 still the biggest Mega in economic terms is
the Boston-to-Washington corridor. In 1961
it was home to about 32 million people; today
its population has risen to 55 million, more
than 17 percent of all Americans. The region
70 generates $242.5 trillion in economic activity,
making it the world's fourth largest economy,
bigger than France or the United Kingdom.
Next in line is Chi-Pitts, the great Midwestern
Mega running from Chicago to Detroit,
75 Cleveland, and Pittsburgh, with $242.3 trillion

in economic activity. Three of the power
centers of the U.S. economy even stretch
beyond American borders: So-Cal runs from
Los Angeles to San Diego across the Mexican
80 border to Tijuana; Tor-Buff-Chester sprawls
from Toronto to Rochester, and Cascadia from
Portland, Oregon, to Vancouver.

Aside from the island-bound financial
center of Greater London, Europe's major
85 economic engines do not **rely** on old borders
to define themselves. The Euro-Lowlands
cuts across four nations: the Netherlands,
Belgium, Germany, and France. The Euro-
Sunbelt stretches from Barcelona to Marseille,
90 attracting people and firms with competitive
costs and the Mediterranean lifestyle. Japan
is less a country than a **network** of linked
Mega-regions, anchored by Greater Tokyo:
indeed, a close look at the light-emissions map
95 shows that its three major Megas may well be
blurring into one super-Mega of more than
100 million people.

While Mega-regions power advanced
economies, they literally define the emerging
100 nations. If you **removed** its Megas, China
would be virtually meaningless as an economic
category. What matters are Shang-King
(Shanghai to Nanjing), with more than 50
million people; Hong-Zen (Hong Kong to
105 Shenzhen), 40 million; Greater Beijing, 36
million. These three Megas account for most
of Chinese economic output, attract most of
its talent, and generate the great majority of
its innovations.

110 Instead of technology helping to spread
economic opportunity and lift many more
boats, economic power is concentrating in
a small number of key regions. It's time for
political and economic leadership to wake
115 up to this new reality. It makes little sense to
dwell on countries anymore, when the real
engines of **survival**, innovation, and growth
are the New Megas.

[3] *exponentially*: extremely rapidly

[4] *hone*: sharpen

[5] *tipping point*: the moment at which a trend reaches its peak and starts to decline

READING COMPREHENSION

Mark each sentence as *T* (true) or *F* (false) according to the information in Reading 1. Correct each false statement in your notebook.

.... 1. Across the globe, nations create economic growth more than regions.

.... 2. Major international institutions such as the United Nations have been systematically collecting information about megacities.

.... 3. There are about 20 megacities scattered around the globe.

.... 4. The biggest mega-region is Chicago to Pittsburgh, in the United States.

.... 5. Mega-regions sometimes ignore borders and include more than one country.

.... 6. The three major Megas in China account for almost all of China's economic power.

.... 7. When older cities get too large, new cities emerge in the middle of nowhere.

.... 8. According to urbanologist Jane Jacobs, people become more productive and creative when they gather together in cities.

READING STRATEGY: Identifying Main Ideas vs. Supporting Details

Writers offer specific details and examples to clarify and support their general ideas. When reading a text, it is helpful to identify both the main ideas and the supporting details and note these in a simple outline form.

A. Read these excerpts from Reading 1. Put a check (✓) next to those that are main ideas.

.... Nations don't spur growth as much as dynamic regions.

.... Today, its population has risen to 55 million.

.... Europe's major economic engines have even less respect for old borders.

.... The New Megas are the real economic organizing units of the world.

.... The global economy takes shape around perhaps 20 great Megas.

.... What matters are Shang-King (Shanghai to Nanjing); Hong-Zen (Hong Kong to Shenzhen); and Greater Beijing.

.... The region generates $242.5 trillion in economic activity.

B. Reading 1 has nine paragraphs. What is the writer's main purpose in each? Write some notes (no sentences necessary) about the focus of each paragraph.

Paragraph 1: *explain idea of "mega," give some examples of megas* ....

Paragraph 2: ....

Paragraph 3: ....

Paragraph 4: ....

Paragraph 5: ....

Paragraph 6: ....

Paragraph 7: ....

Paragraph 8: ....

Paragraph 9: ....

C. Now, in your own words, summarize the main idea of the entire article:

....

....

STEP I VOCABULARY ACTIVITIES: Word Level

A *network* is "an interconnected or interrelated chain, group, or system." There are various types of *networks*. The noun form is frequently combined with other nouns to make collocations, for example, a *computer network* or a *television network*.

The verb form of *network* means to "create social communication channels and mutual support systems." People network to advance their careers or to improve their social lives.

A. Match the type of network with its example. Use your dictionary to help you understand new words. Compare answers with a partner.

.... **1.** MTV or CNN   **a.** computer network

.... **2.** a company's intranet   **b.** transportation network

.... **3.** the Bill and Melinda Gates Foundation   **c.** television network

.... **4.** the Paris metro   **d.** communications network

.... **5.** the human central nervous system   **e.** job network

.... **6.** friends you meet through other friends   **f.** neural network

.... **7.** satellite mobile phones   **g.** social network

.... **8.** people you work with   **h.** philanthropic network

The word *migrate* means "move from one area to another." It is usually used to describe the seasonal movement of all types of animals.

Salmon **migrate** *to their birthplace every spring to lay their eggs.*

Note: *Migrate* is the root for two other words you probably know that describe movement of people from one country to another: *immigrate* (to move into another country) and *emigrate* (to move out of your own country).

B. With a partner, think of three species (type of animal, bird, fish, or insect) that migrate, and then discuss what you know about them. For each species, consider these things:

- departure point
- destination
- length of trip in time and distance
- how it finds its way
- the purpose of the migration

1. Species: ....

Notes: ....

....

2. Species: ....

Notes: ....

....

3. Species: ....

Notes: ....

....

C. Complete the sentences about megacities using the target vocabulary in the box. Use each item one time. The synonyms in parentheses can help you.

communications   network
define   rely on
global   survival
migrate

1. Megacities form a vast expanse of trade, transport, ... ,
(message systems)
innovation, and talent.

2. The maps make it clear that the .... economy takes shape
(worldwide)
around perhaps 20 great Megas.

3. Mega-regions compose a major part of advanced economies and actually
.... several emerging nations.
   (give complete form to)

4. Japan is less a country than a .... of Mega-regions, anchored by
   (interconnected system)
   Greater Tokyo.

5. When many people .... to one place, they all become more
   (move)
   productive.

6. The .... of megacities will depend on their ability to adapt to the
   (continued existence)
   needs of their people and the environment.

7. Although many cities .... imports for much of their food, fast-
   (count on)
   growing megacities are often incapable of organizing the food imports they need.

D. What are some sources for these items? Think globally and locally. Discuss your answers in a small group and choose the three most significant sources for each item.

1. information about traffic conditions
2. information for an essay on electricity usage
3. pollution
4. creativity

STEP II VOCABULARY ACTIVITIES: Sentence Level

E. *Status* has several meanings. Write your own definitions based on these example sentences. Do not use your dictionary. Be prepared to compare and discuss your definitions with a partner. You may check your dictionaries afterward.

1. The application asked for his age, his place of birth, his marital status, and a lot of other personal details.

   ....

   ....

2. Celebrities often have a higher status in society than regular people.

   ....

   ....

3. The foreman reported to the committee on the status of the construction of the new administration building. He said it should be finished within six months.

   ....

   ....

The verb *rely* is actually a verb phrase because it always takes the preposition *on*. There are two typical structures for this verb phrase: "*Rely on* someone (or something) *for* something" is one:

> City planners **rely on** experts <u>for data</u> on population growth, traffic patterns, and ecological impact.

"*Rely on* someone (or something) *to do* something" is another:

> As cities become more crowded, residents **rely on** public transportation more and more <u>to get around town</u>.

Word Form Chart			
Noun	Verb	Adjective	Adverb
reliance relying (gerund) reliability	rely (on)	reliable unreliable	reliably

F. Complete these sentences using a form of *rely*. Be sure to use the verb phrase *rely on* where appropriate.

1. He .... his parents for money.

2. She always does what she promises to do. She is completely ....

3. He rarely asks for help. He believes that self-.. is better than .... on others.

4. His new car often breaks down. He can't depend on it; it is very

   ....

5. She .... her friends to tell her the truth.

6. If you want to leave at 2:30, tell Mika to be here at 2:00. She is

   .... late for everything!

7. This car was rated #1 in .... and safety by automotive analysts.

Now write four sentences of your own using four different forms of *rely*.

1. ....

2. ....

3. ....

4. ....

BEFORE YOU READ

Read these questions. Be prepared to discuss your answers.

1. Where do the people in your city get all the food they need? What do they do with all their garbage?

2. What particular ecological challenges does your city have to deal with? What special policies or regulations are in place to help the city cope with these challenges? What do you think should be done to cope with them?

3. What impact do big cities have on the environment? Give examples to support your ideas.

READ

This article from *New Scientist* magazine discusses the ecological advantages of urban living.

Ecopolis Now

Forget the rural idyll. Urban living may be the best way to save the planet.

A hundred years ago, the largest city in the world was London, with a population of 6.5 million. Today it is dwarfed by Tokyo. With barely a quarter the population of London a
5 century ago, the Tokyo metropolitan area has since mushroomed to 34 million, propelling it to first place in the global city league table. Tokyo's phenomenal growth is largely due to a single factor: migration from the countryside to
10 the city. It is just one of many to have overtaken London, which with a population of 7.5 million today doesn't even make the top 20.

This rural-to-urban migration can now be seen in scores of cities around the globe. And it
15 has brought us to a pivotal moment in human history. In 1900, most people lived in the countryside, with a little over 10 percent of the world's population living in cities. From next year, the UN Population Division predicts that
20 for the first time in history, more people will live in cities than in the country, and the biggest growth will be in "megacities," with populations over 10 million.

The meteoric growth of megacities—there
25 are now 20 in total—has brought with it huge environmental and social problems. Cities occupy just two percent of the land surface of the Earth but consume three-quarters of the resources that are used up each year, expelling
30 the half-digested remains in clouds of greenhouse gases, billions of tons of solid waste, and rivers of toxic sewage. Their inhabitants are making ruinous demands on soils and water supplies for food and on forests for timber and paper.

35 Returning the world's population to the countryside isn't an option. Dividing up the planet into plots of land on which we could all survive self-sufficiently would create its own natural disasters, not to mention being highly
40 unlikely to ever happen. If we are to protect what is left of nature, and meet the demand to improve the quality of living for the world's developing nations, a new form of city living is the only option. The size of a city creates
45 economies of scale for things such as energy generation, recycling, and public transport. It should even be possible for cities to partly feed themselves. Far from being parasites on the world, cities could hold the key to sustainable
50 living for the world's booming population—if they are built right.

Fortunately, governments, planners, architects, and engineers are beginning to wake up to this idea, and are dreaming up new ways to
55 green the megacities. Their approaches rely on two main principles: recycle whatever possible and remove as many cars as possible. So as well as developing energy-efficient buildings, emphasis is being placed on increasing the use
60 of public transport and redesigning how cities are organized to integrate work and living areas into a single neighborhood, rather than separating cities into residential, commercial, and industrial zones.

65 The big ideas are still being defined, but many cities already have showcase[1] eco-projects. For example, at the new home of Melbourne city council in Australia, hanging gardens and water fountains cool the air, wind
70 turbines and solar cells generate up to 85 percent of the electricity used in the building, and rooftop rainwater collectors supply 70 percent of its water needs. In Berlin, Germany's new Reichstag parliament building
75 cut its carbon dioxide emissions by 94 percent by relying on carbon-neutral vegetable oil as its energy source. In San Diego, California, garbage trucks run on methane **extracted** from the landfills they deliver to. In Austria,
80 1500 free bicycles have been distributed across Vienna. Reykjavik in Iceland is among the pioneers of hydrogen-powered public transport, and Shanghai is subsidizing the installation of 100,000 rooftop solar panels.
85 The Chinese city is also about to put many of these ideas to the test by creating the first purpose-built eco-city from scratch.

Planners and architects now agree that to improve the social and environmental
90 condition of cities the top priority is to cut car use. They say zero-emission cars running on electricity or burning hydrogen are not enough. "Automobiles still require massive networks of streets, freeways, and parking
95 structures to serve congested cities and far-flung suburbs," says Richard Register, founder of the nonprofit campaigning organization EcoCity Builders in Oakland, California. What is needed is a wholesale rethink of how
100 new cities are laid out—and how existing ones expand—to minimize the need for cars in the first place. One way of achieving this is to build cities with multiple centers where people live close to their work in high-rise
105 blocks that are also near public transport hubs. In parts of the world this is already taking shape.

While planners look at how to cut back the energy consumption of big cities, at the other
110 end of the scale are shanty towns—organically evolved and self-built by millions of people in the developing world without a planner in sight. These shanties meet many of the ideals of eco-city designers. They are high-density
115 but low-rise; their lanes and alleys are largely pedestrianized; and many of their inhabitants recycle waste materials from the wider city. From a purely ecological **perspective**, shanties and their inhabitants are a good
120 example of the new, green urban metabolism[2]. Despite their sanitary and security failings, they often have a social vibrancy and sound ecological status that gets lost in most planned urban environments.

125 So perhaps something can be taken from the chaos and decentralized spontaneity embodied in shanties, and combined with the planned infrastructure of a designed eco-city. Cities built without extensive high
130 rises can still be dense enough to make life without a car profitable, and they can retain the economies of scale needed for the new metabolism built around efficient recycling of everything from sewage to sandwich wrappers.
135 At the same time, they need to remain flexible enough for people to adapt them to the way they want to live.

---

[1] *showcase*: publicized in a positive way
[2] *metabolism*: way of using energy

READING COMPREHENSION

Mark each sentence as *T* (true) or *F* (false) according to the information in Reading 2. Correct each false statement in your notebook.

.... **1.** Urban migration is a global trend.

.... **2.** Megacities have brought about few ecological or social problems.

.... **3.** Returning to the countryside is a good alternative for modern city dwellers if megacities create significant problems.

.... **4.** Governments and planners know that megacities need to become more ecology-minded.

.... **5.** The top priority of urban planners is to decrease car use.

.... **6.** Planners are trying to minimize the need for cars by rethinking the way cities are laid out.

.... **7.** From a purely ecological perspective, unplanned shanty towns are possible models for the future.

.... **8.** Megacities are not expected to grow much more than they already have.

READING STRATEGY: Outlining a Text

Reread the article on pages 25–26. As you read each paragraph, think about the writer's main purpose. Then, create an outline below by identifying the main ideas and supporting details.

Paragraph 1, Main Idea: ....

   Supporting detail: ....

   Supporting detail: ....

Paragraph 2, Main Idea: ....

   Supporting detail: ....

   Supporting detail: ....

Paragraph 3, Main Idea: ....

   Supporting detail: ....

   Supporting detail: ....

Paragraph 4, Main Idea: ....

   Supporting detail: ....

   Supporting detail: ....

continued

Paragraph 5, Main Idea: ....

    Supporting detail: ....

    Supporting detail: ....

Paragraph 6, Main Idea: ....

    Supporting detail: ....

    Supporting detail: ....

Paragraph 7, Main Idea: ....

    Supporting detail: ....

    Supporting detail: ....

Paragraph 8, Main Idea: ....

    Supporting detail: ....

    Supporting detail: ....

Paragraph 9, Main Idea: ....

    Supporting detail: ....

    Supporting detail: ....

Now, in your own words, summarize the main idea of the entire article:

....

STEP I VOCABULARY ACTIVITIES: Word Level

A. With a partner, complete the word form chart. Use your dictionary to help you. Then, complete the sentences that follow using the correct form of *communicate*.

Word Form Chart for *challenge*		
Noun	Verb	Adjective
1. (a person): 2. (thing, singular): 3. (thing, plural):	communicate	1. 2. communicable

1. He talked openly and honestly about the problem. He was very

    ....

2. She speaks clearly and enthusiastically. She's an effective ....

3. Regular .... is an important part of any business or social
   relationship.

4. Computers and cell phones have completely changed modern

   ....

5. The committee members disagree, but they must .... with each other in order to reach a compromise and settle the issue.

6. Some diseases are passed genetically from parent to child. Others are ....— they pass from one person to another through contact.

B. Complete these sentences from another *New Scientist* article, "Urban Appetite," about food and the ecology of cities, using the target vocabulary in the box. Use each item one time.

communications	globe	sources
defined	major	status
despite	network	survived
extracting	rely	

1. The megacity is .... as a city with a population of more than
   (specifically described)
   10 million.

2. Sometime around 1940, New York City was the first to reach megacity

   ....
   (rank or standing)

3. Extensive transport networks, the boom in cheap ...., and
   (technological message systems)
   cultural changes in work and living have contributed to the rise of megacities.

4. Feeding a city is not easy. Unable or unwilling to .... on distant
   (depend)
   .... for food, many cities are substantially feeding themselves.
   (supply origins)

5. In the early 1990s, the Bosnian capital of Sarajevo .... a siege by
   (stayed alive)
   cultivating its wasteland.

6. Water managers believe that governments should make city sewage safe for

   irrigation and fertilization by .... disease-causing pathogens
   (taking out)
   while leaving the nutrients.

7. "Eco-cities must be farming cities," says Jac Smit, president of UAN, the Urban

   Agriculture .... run by the United Nations Development
   (interconnected group)
   Program.

8. .... the .... social and ecological challenges
   (even though there are)   *(very big)*
   they present, megacities around the .... can and must be jointly
   (earth)
   adapted to both people and planet.

C. Give three examples of these things. Discuss your answers with a partner. Why do you think your examples are *major*?

1. a major artist: ....

....

2. a major river: ....

....

3. a major catastrophe: ....

....

4. a major scientific achievement: ....

....

5. a major improvement in human life: ....

....

The word *major* also has an academic meaning. As a noun, it means "a field of study chosen as an academic specialty." It can also describe a student specializing in such studies.

He finally decided on urban planning as a major.

He is an architecture major.

As a verb, *major* means "to pursue academic studies in a particular subject."

*She is **majoring** in mathematics.*

Some students major in two subjects. This is called *double majoring* and students are called *double majors*.

He is double majoring in political science and geography.

D. Imagine your friends ask you for advice about what major they should choose. For each profession, which major(s) would you recommend? Discuss your reasons in a small group.

1. humanitarian aid worker

2. factory pollution inspector

3. tax collector

4. executive assistant

5. magazine editor

6. television producer

STEP II VOCABULARY ACTIVITIES: Sentence Level

Despite is a preposition used to show contrasts or opposites of action, thought, or expectation.

Despite *their sanitary and security failings, shanty towns often have social vibrancy and sound ecological status.*

You can also use the phrase *the fact that* to connect clauses.

Despite <u>*the fact that*</u> *the rise of regions has been apparent for more than a decade, no one has collected systematic information on them.*

Note: *In spite of* has the exact same meaning as *despite* and can be used in the same grammatical structures.

In spite of *their sanitary and security failings, shanty towns often have social vibrancy and sound ecological status.*

In spite of <u>*the fact that*</u> *the rise of regions has been apparent for more than a decade, no one has collected systematic information on them.*

E. Write four sentences featuring information you have learned about cities. Use the words in parentheses in your sentences.

1. (despite)

....

....

2. (despite)

....

....

3. (despite the fact that)

....

....

4. (in spite of / in spite of the fact that)

....

....

F. Read the definitions of *perspective*. Decide which meaning applies to each of the sample sentences. Then, rewrite the sample sentences without using the target word.

> **a.** creating the appearance of objects in depth on a flat surface
> **b.** the ability to view things in their true relation or relative importance
> **c.** the viewpoint or position of a particular person or group

.... 1. It was difficult for the mayor to maintain a realistic perspective of the traffic problem after she was in a car accident.

....

....

.... 2. The students are using a new computer program that depicts city streets and buildings in perspective.

....

....

.... 3. From the environmental group's perspective, any law allowing cars into the city center should be opposed as unsafe and unhealthy for citizens.

....

....

G. Self-Assessment Review: Go back to page 17 and reassess your knowledge of the target vocabulary. How has your understanding of the words changed? What words do you feel most comfortable with now?

WRITING AND DISCUSSION TOPICS

1. Think about the career of urban planning. What kinds of training, experience, and knowledge do you think an urban planner should possess today? What should someone interested in urban planning major in? What difficulties will urban planners of the future face?

2. Should the environmental issues raised by megacities be dealt with on a city level, country level, regional level, or global level?

3. Describe the megacity of the future (100 years from now) from the perspective of a resident of the city. Include both good and bad aspects.

4. Describe your current social network. How and when did you become part of it? What other networks do you rely on for communicating or getting around? Have you ever done any networking for school, work, or social reasons?

5. What is (or will be) your major? How did you (will you) decide what subject to major in? Do you think it is better to major in something you enjoy or something that will help you get a good job?

IN THE PUBLIC EYE

In this unit, you will

- ➲ read about some public art exhibits and the issues they raise for artists and communities.
- ➲ learn how to skim a reading for main ideas and make predictions before you read.
- ➲ learn how to scan a reading after you read it to check if your predictions were correct.
- ➲ increase your understanding of the target academic words for this unit:

comment	fund	inspect	mutual	rational
criteria	goal	interpret	ongoing	topic
ethnic	guideline	legislate	policy	

SELF-ASSESSMENT OF TARGET WORDS

Think carefully about how well you know each target word in this unit. Then, write it in the appropriate column in the chart.

I have never seen the word before.	I have seen the word but am not sure what it means.	I understand the word when I see or hear it in a sentence.	I have tried to use the word, but I am not sure I am using it correctly.	I use the word with confidence in either speaking *or* writing.	I use the word with confidence, both in speaking *and* writing.

BEFORE YOU READ

Read these questions. Discuss your answers in a small group.

1. Have you been to an art gallery or art museum? What did you like or not like about that experience?

2. What is different about the experience of seeing art outside, compared with going to an art gallery or museum?

3. How would you define "public art"? What types of things would this include? What, do you think, is its purpose?

READING STRATEGY: Skimming and Making Predictions

Pre-reading skills can help you read more quickly and understand important ideas more completely. One important pre-reading skill is skimming for main ideas and making predictions. "Skimming" means reading quickly, looking for important ideas, but not focusing on every word you see, and not reading entire sentences.

Follow these steps to preview and make predictions about Reading 1.

First, read the title and the subtitle and look at the picture. Write a guess about the topic of the reading.

I think this article will be about ....

Second, read the first paragraph and the last paragraph. Do you think your first guess was correct? If not, write a new guess, or add more specific information to your first guess.

I think this article will be about ....

Next, look at the headings (the words in bold type) that begin each section of the article. *Don't read the paragraphs—only the headings.* For each heading, think of one or two questions that you think the section might answer. Try to ask about the most important ideas you think each section might discuss.

Heading 1: Benefits for businesses and charities

   Question 1a: *What are the benefits for businesses?* ....

   Question 1b: .... ?

Heading 2: ....

   Question 2a: .... ?

   Question 2b: .... ?

Heading 3: ....

    Question 3a: ....?

    Question 3b: ....?

Finally, make a guess about the main idea of the article.

    Main idea: ....

As you read the article, think about the questions you thought of. How well did you anticipate the information in each section?

READ

Reading 1 contains many puns. A pun is a way of playing with language to make a joke. A pun is made by combining two words—one with the meaning that you intend, and one that is related to a specific topic.

For example, in the title of the article, "moonicipal" is a pun. The word *municipal* means "public" or "related to a city," and *moo* is the sound that a cow makes.

Because the article is about cows, there are many puns using cow-related words. As you read, notice the other puns the author makes. They have been underlined for your reference.

This article is about a public art display that took place in Edinburgh, Scotland.

The Best of <u>Moonicipal</u> Art

Cows Will Parade Across Edinburgh, May 15–23.

If you're reading this in Edinburgh, a word of warning. At some point on Monday morning you might come face to face with a brightly colored fiberglass cow. Then, later in the day, you might
5 see another. And another. Do not be alarmed. You are not losing your mind. You have simply walked into the middle of the largest **ongoing** public art event in the world.

Since it started in 1998 in Zurich, Cow Parade
10 has appeared in cities across the world, from New York to Tokyo, Prague to Sao Paulo. More than 3,000 bovines[1], designed by artists, celebrities, and community groups, have grazed around the world's most famous landmarks, before being
15 auctioned to help **fund** charity groups.

Under cover of darkness on Sunday night, 94

Cow Parade in Edinburgh

cows will take up their stations at Edinburgh landmarks, as well as some more <u>unmoosual</u> spots. Night <u>Moo</u> on Blair Street will glow in the
20 dark. Cow for the Castle has the city's famous skyline on her side, while a specially modeled <u>Bravemoo</u> stands on her hind legs and wears an **ethnic** costume, in the manner of William "Braveheart" Wallace, the Scottish folk hero.

---

[1] *bovine*: cow, or related to cows

"Never before has Edinburgh seen such a sight," says gallery director Richard Demarco. "I think it's great that you don't have to build a multi-million-pound new gallery to house what is in fact an extremely large-scale city-transforming exhibition. I'm going to enjoy them while they're here. I recognize a life-enhancing exhibition when I see one."

Benefits for businesses and charities

For the idea of the cow as art object, we must thank Zurich window-dresser Walter Knapp, who came up with the concept of a fiberglass herd to boost business in the city. His artist son Pascal was tasked with designing a "unique three-dimensional canvas" for artists, which was, well, cow-shaped. His three cow designs—standing, reclining and grazing—are now mass-produced by a Polish factory to meet Cow Parade demands around the world.

The Zurich cows achieved Knapp's **goal**: they brought visitors to the city in droves, and the visitors increased the income of local businesses. The following year, Cows on Parade was unveiled in Chicago, where it was proclaimed the most successful public art exhibition in the history of the city. Now, Cow Parade is a private company that has perfected its idea, limiting itself to several cities a year in order to retain its prestige (this year is the turn of Edinburgh, Lisbon, Paris, Budapest and Boston). Businesses pay up to £5,000 to sponsor a cow, though there is a reduced rate for commoonity groups.

While the show is free, the retail and service sectors benefit enormously from the increased tourism. Then, at the end of the show, instead of puzzling over what to do with hundreds of life-size fiberglass cows, which aren't a novelty anymore, Cow Parade auctions them for charity. In Edinburgh, 70 percent of proceeds will be divided between the OneCity Trust, which tackles social exclusion, and VetAid, which works to alleviate poverty by sustainable farming in developing countries.

Artists and sponsors

For the artists involved, designing a cow is a process of negotiating **guidelines** with the sponsor, who generally wants their animal to reflect a **topic** related to their business. According to the Cow Parade **policy**, logos and brands are not allowed. Bad puns involving bovine vocabulary, however, are actively encouraged.

Edinburgh artist Clare Waddle has designed An Udder Cowch for the Omni Centre, a careful fusion of her own playfully kitsch[2] artistic ideas and the **criteria** of the sponsor. The cow, one of very few reclining cows in Edinburgh, reflects the Centre's desire to promote itself as a "home from home" with a built-in couch and standard lamp. Waddle believes the project has **mutual** benefit for artists and sponsors.

"When I submitted my designs I was working on an exhibition for the Amber Roome Gallery, and I was interested to see if I could take some of the concepts I'd been working with for the last year into the cow. I presented drawings to the Omni Centre and we came to an agreement. I took their needs into consideration from the start, and they liked what I did."

Sense of humor brings success

One thing's for certain, normally straight-laced Edinburgh is in for a shock when the hooves[3] hit the streets. Demarco chuckles, suggesting that the city's famous conservative, religious forefathers could never have imagined such a thing.

But as well as bringing people and art together, he believes it's a great antidote to the over-seriousness of some contemporary art. He believes that art needs a sense of humor, and sees the cows' silliness as the answer to the

---

[2] *kitsch*: appealing to popular tastes, uncultured
[3] *hoof* (pl. *hooves*): the hard part of the foot of cows, horses, and other animals

depressing, self-important modern art that he believes most young artists seem to favor.

While the success of the idea has led to spin-offs using other animals—whales in Connecticut, pigs in Cincinnati, lizards in
115 Orlando, moose in Toronto, bears in Berlin—the cow continues to reign supreme. "There is something loveable about a cow," **comments** Demarco. "A kind of motherly touch. They are a symbol of civilization. Thank goodness we don't
120 have 94 bulls—that would have been quite a different thing."

READING COMPREHENSION

A. Circle the best answer to the questions. Skim the article to help you find the answers.

1. What does the public art display in Edinburgh consist of?
   a. 94 live cows standing at famous landmarks throughout the city
   b. Statues of whales, pigs, lizards, moose, and bears from around the world
   c. Almost 100 painted statues of cows placed in different spots
   d. A reclining cow with a lamp and couch, advertising the Omni Center

2. Why was the first Cow Parade created?
   a. To give people a life-changing experience
   b. To help young artists try out new ideas
   c. To bring a sense of humor to modern art
   d. To increase the income of local businesses

3. What happens to the cows when the exhibit is over?
   a. They are given back to the artists.
   b. They are sold to raise money for charity.
   c. They are used to promote businesses.
   d. They are exhibited in other cities.

4. Why does Demarco like the Cow Parade?
   a. He approves of giving funds to charity.
   b. He is interested in businesses making a profit.
   c. He admires the "unique, three-dimensional canvas."
   d. He enjoys the silly approach to modern art.

B. Did you understand all the puns? With a partner, skim the article for each underlined pun and explain it to each other as you understand it.

STEP I VOCABULARY ACTIVITIES: Word Level

A. Match the words on the left with its meaning or meanings on the right. Then, for the words with more than one meaning, circle the meaning that is used in Reading 1. Compare your answers with a partner.

.... 1. ongoing	**a.** rules
.... 2. fund	**b.** to mention (*v*), statement (*n*)
.... 3. ethnic	**c.** to finance (*v*), money (*n*)
.... 4. goal	**d.** objective
.... 5. guidelines	**e.** in progress, incomplete
.... 6. topic	**f.** subject
.... 7. mutual	**g.** national, racial
.... 8. comment	**h.** shared

B. Read these sentences about city public art programs. For each sentence, cross out the one word or phrase in parentheses with a different meaning from the other three choices. Rewrite the sentence in your notebook using one of the choices. Compare your answers with a partner.

1. Many cities have (*continuing / ongoing / momentary / long-term*) public art programs that produce new works on a regular basis.

2. Some cities have a (*rule / policy / law / limit*) requiring that a certain percentage of the budget be used to fund public art.

3. In order to receive government support, proposals must follow certain (*guidelines / styles / rules / specifications*) for public art.

4. Local governments use many different (*factors / resources / considerations / criteria*) when deciding what public art projects to fund.

5. The (*problem / goal / aim / purpose*) of local government is to (*fund / enable / support / repair*) new public art projects that provide opportunities for community involvement.

6. Public art projects are successful because local government and members of the community feel a (*common / ongoing / mutual / two-way*) responsibility to keep them clean and attractive, so the two groups cooperate in maintaining them.

7. Some public art (*comments on / refers to / speaks to / covers up*) problems in the local area, while other exhibits have no political message.

8. Some public art promotes understanding of and respect for diversity. For example, an artwork can express (*cultural / ethnic / national / selfish*) pride.

C. Read this passage about the different kinds of public art and their significance to local communities. Fill in the blanks using the target vocabulary in the box. The synonyms in parentheses can help you.

commented	goals	policy
criteria	guidelines	topic
ethnic	mutual	
funded	ongoing	

People have different viewpoints when they discuss the .... of
(1. *aims*)
public art. However, the most important .... for deciding whether
(2. *factors*)
something is public art are its availability and accessibility to the community.

Sometimes, city government requests a public art project. Often, cities have a
"percent for art" .... with .... showing how to use
(3. *rule*)   (4. *recommendations*)
a certain percentage of the budget for art. Some public art projects are initiated by
artists. The artist decides on a .... for a project then convinces the
(5. *subject*)
community and a sponsor that it is a worthwhile project.

In other cases, public art projects are started by communities that want
to improve the appearance of their neighborhoods, for example by using
.... art to celebrate the culture of local residents.
(6. *cultural*)
Public art has many different forms and functions, both when it is created and in
its .... existence. A mural is a good example. The City of Seattle has
(7. *continuing*)
.... more murals than any other kind of public art project. Murals
(8. *given money for*)
have been painted many places, including walls, bus shelters, and even a trash can.

No matter where it is located, however, a mural has far-reaching effects.
Glenna B. Avila, former director of Los Angeles's City Wide Mural Project
.... that murals are about the .... respect and
(9. *said*)   (10. *shared*)
affection between people and their cities, with artists from the community taking
responsibility for their visual and physical environment, and, in the process,
changing neighborhoods, decreasing vandalism, and creating new artists in the
community.

> *Criteria* is the plural form of *criterion*. The plural form is far more commonly used than the singular form.
>
> *Criteria* means "the standards that you use when you make a decision or form an opinion." For example, to decide what kind of car to buy, the usual criteria are price, size, gas mileage, safety, and whether it has extra things you might want, like a CD player.

D. Work in a small group to decide the three most important criteria for deciding these things.

1. the kind of apartment or house you want to live in

....

2. the kind of person you would like to date or marry

....

3. the best kind of animal for a pet

....

4. the best modern musician

....

5. the most important invention of all time

....

STEP II VOCABULARY ACTIVITIES: Sentence Level

E. Read these sentences about a public art project in Dubai. Rephrase them in your notebook using the target vocabulary in parentheses.

1. "Art for everyone" is the purpose of a public art display in Dubai called the Celebration of the Arabian Horse, which will raise money for local and international charities. (*goal, fund*)

   "Art for everyone" is the goal of Dubai's current major public art exhibition, the Celebration of the Arabian Horse, which will fund local and international charities.

2. The display features life-size Arabian horse sculptures in high-profile locations in Dubai and has the same artistic focus as the "Pride of Arabia" now in process, which includes 21 small Arabian horse sculptures at a local gallery. (*mutual, ongoing*)

3. Godolphin has funded several international artists from different cultural backgrounds to create their own interpretations of the theme of Arabian horses, for display in Dubai's public areas. (*ethnic, topic*)

4. Patricia McGourty Palmer, Director of Dubai-based ArtWorks and founder of the project, said that each artist brought a unique and creative interpretation to the image of the Arabian Horse. (*comment*)

To *fund* means "to give money for a project or a business." A *fund* is an account that exists to give money to a certain person or purpose. *Funds* (plural only) is a synonym for money. *Funding* is money that a project or organization receives to help with its work.

*City governments often **fund** public art projects.*

*Many cities have a special **fund** for public art projects.*

*Many organizations that produce public art do not have a lot of **funds**.*

*These organizations rely on **funding** from charitable organizations and local government.*

F. In your notebook, restate these sentences so that they include a form of *fund*. Share your sentences in a small group. How many different ways were you able to use *fund* in each case?

1. A new public art display in Shanghai is sponsored by the Shanghai Cultural Development Foundation and Shanghai Urban Sculpture Committee Office. The exhibit includes more than 200 sculptures by 70 artists from around the world.

2. Even people who don't have any money for artistic entertainment can see the display because it is free.

3. Liu Jianhua, a sculpture professor at Shanghai University, is pleased to see that the government is now providing financial support for public art.

4. In the past, Liu commented that there have not been many sculpture displays in town due to insufficient space and money.

5. If this show is successful, perhaps the government will create an account to generate money for public art.

6. Government contributions would certainly help the city to improve the quality of its public art.

G. Read the explanations and descriptions of public art in Activities B and C. Imagine that you are a journalist who is going to interview your local city government about its policy for funding public art, the history of public art in your city, and current public art displays. Prepare interview questions using the cues provided. (After you write your questions, be prepared to conduct the interview with a partner in a role play.)

1. which/criteria

   Which criteria do you use to evaluate proposals for public art?

2. what/fund
3. do/ethnic
4. what/topic
5. what/guidelines
6. who/policy
7. what/goal
8. when/ongoing

BEFORE YOU READ

Read these questions. Discuss your answers in a small group.

1. Have you ever seen art that you did not think should be considered art? Why did you think so?

2. Who should make decisions about what is art? What criteria should they use?

3. Is it possible for art to be bad, or must anything that is considered art also be considered good art?

READING STRATEGY

The headings in an article are very helpful for skimming. But many articles do not contain headings. You can use other methods to skim articles without headings. Then, you can make predictions to help prepare yourself for the information you are going to read.

Follow these steps to preview and make predictions about Reading 2.

First, read the title and look at the picture. Write a guess about the topic of the reading.

   I think this article will be about ....

Second, read the first paragraph and the last paragraph. Do you think your first guess was correct? If not, write a new guess, or add more specific information to your first guess.

   I think this article will be about ....

Next, look at the first sentence of each paragraph. *Don't read the whole paragraph— only the first sentence.* For each sentence, think of one or two questions that you think the paragraph might answer and write them in your notebook. Try to ask about the most important ideas you think each paragraph might discuss.

   Paragraph 1: Do people like this public art display?

Finally, make a guess about the main idea of the article.

   Main idea: ....

As you read the article, think about the questions you thought of. How well did you anticipate the information in each paragraph?

Reading 2 contains many puns that center around animals and their characteristics. As you read, underline the puns you find.

This article, by Thomas Vinciguerra, appeared in *The Philadelphia Inquirer* newspaper. Vinciguerra questions whether public displays such as Cow Parade can truly be considered art.

Going to the Dogs

As most area residents know, a collection of 30 brightly painted, oversize fiberglass statues of Nipper, the canine symbol of the Victor Talking Machine Co., has been on display throughout
5 Moorestown[1] since June. Officially titled "Nipper 2005," the ongoing installation has been well-received. But is it art?

Nipper, then and now

Ever since Chicago unveiled the 360 bovine sculptures that made up "Cows on
10 Parade" in 1999, many American cities have displayed their own exhibits of brightly painted animals. Underscoring their playful nature, the projects often bear painfully clever names—hence, Cincinnati's "Big Pig Gig"
15 (425 swine), Buffalo's "Herd About Buffalo" (150 bison), Orlando's "LizArt" (200 geckos), and Louisville's "Gallapalooza" (200 horses). The trend seems unstoppable. This summer, "Crabtown Project" (nearly 200 crabs)
20 descended on Baltimore. Right now, Zion, Illinois, is hosting "Swarm and the City"
(81 bees). For many in the fine arts community, this is a case of kitsch gone wild.

"It's the scourge[2] of Western civilization,"
25 said Tom Eccles, former director of the Public Art Fund, a nonprofit New York group, who says that he can't find a **rational** reason for the success of these projects. Art, he argues, is more than putting paint on cute fiberglass
30 animals. While he stops short of asking local government to **legislate** against the displays, he believes they should be discouraged. Eccles argues that it is ridiculous to call these animal parades art, and that doing so should be
35 considered fraud. Betsy Fahlman, a professor of art history at Arizona State University, mildly disagrees. She does not believe that the displays are evil, but she also does not see them as great masterpieces. Instead,
40 she describes the animals as short-lived, humorous, and unsophisticated. *Inquirer* art critic Edward J. Sozanski commented, "For reasons I can't begin to fathom, the animals appear to be an unusually effective fund-
45 raising gimmick[3]." The problem, he believes, is that they encourage low standards for artists and for funding public art. He and others in the art world are bothered by seeing people respond so well to something unoriginal and
50 temporary, especially in cities that produce so much top-quality art.

Yet the fiberglass phenomenon remains wildly popular. Superficially, at least, the reasons are obvious. Most ordinary folks,
55 children especially, find the sculptures

[1] *Moorestown, New Jersey*: a suburb of Philadelphia, Pennsylvania
[2] *scourge*: something that causes great suffering
[3] *gimmick*: a trick used to get people's attention

just plain fun. They're relatively cheap, so corporate patrons can easily sponsor local artists to decorate them. Because they are usually displayed for only a few months, they aren't around long enough to become eyesores. And when their time is up, they're auctioned off for charity, civic institutions, or other worthy causes. Moorestown's Nipper sculptures are due to be sold off on Sunday to benefit several community groups. But the big reason animal art has exploded is that it draws people and money to downtown commercial districts, supplying many stores with a badly needed economic jolt. "Cow Parade" yielded $200 million and two million tourists for Chicago, according to some estimates. The roughly one million visitors who came to Cincinnati to **inspect** its "Big Pig Gig" generated more than $124 million in merchant sales.

Mike Hurley, the owner of Fiberglass Farm, a casting company in Belfast, Maine, pointed out that these projects bring together artists, communities, families, and businesses around a mutual interest, which has resulted in success for the displays. Of course, "success" can be evaluated according to many different criteria. The cultural critics deride animal art in part because the statues often have little to do with their communities. The topic of the "Ewe Revue" (43 sheep) in Rochester, Mich., was difficult for most people to connect to the local area. Organizers were inspired by the city's former Western Knitting Mill, which was once among the world's leading wool suppliers. The Moorestown Nippers have a rather stronger connection to their site. The founder of the Victor Co. and the owner of the American rights to "His Master's Voice," the painting that immortalized Nipper, was Eldridge Johnson, who settled in Moorestown after establishing his company in nearby Camden.

Redundancy is another issue. At least 20 cities have had cow parades. Both Kankakee County, Ill., and Raleigh, N.C., have sported wolves. After the success of Cincinnati's pig gig, Peoria, Ill., and Seattle, Wa., responded with porcine[4] projects of their own. "These plastic animals are supposed to generate civic or regional identity," said Erika Doss, author of *Spirit Poles and Flying Pigs: Public Art and Cultural Democracy in American Communities* (Smithsonian Institution Press, 1995). But Doss believes the displays fail to accomplish that goal because they are so similar to each other. Doss, who teaches art history at the University of Colorado at Boulder, also **interprets** the rise in animal art as resulting from the death of individual artistic expression. "I think it's boring, this lack of risk-taking," she said. "Let's see something more interesting."

Anne Pasternak, president and artistic director of Creative Time, a New York-based nonprofit arts group, is concerned that the cities with these art displays have wonderful artists who are not being given the opportunity to do work that does not involve cute animals. Many painters and sculptors, however, have embraced animal art—not as an end in itself, but as a stepping-stone to other projects. Zora Janosova, a 35-year-old muralist in Stamford, Conn., has decorated cows in Atlanta, Ga., birds in Hyattsville, Md., and pandas in Washington, D.C. She has found that these pieces have helped to evoke interest in her own original work. "When I'm showing my portfolio, people react very nicely to it," she said.

If anything, animal art is diversifying, into the realm of the plant kingdom and inanimate objects. Atlantic City, N.J., has put up "Beacons by the Sea" (73 lighthouses); Bloomington, Ill., celebrated its 150th birthday with a bumper crop of "Corn

---

[4] *porcine*: relating to pigs

on the Curb" (29 ears); and Cleveland has offered "GuitarMania" (90 giant Fender Stratocasters). Last year, New York City let
145 loose 300 giant apples for—you guessed it—the "Big Apple Fest."

"I'm completely torn," said Tom Finkelpearl, the director of the Queens (N.Y.) Museum of Art and the author of *Dialogues in Public*
150 *Art* (MIT Press, 2001). "Most people in the public art community think these works give public art a bad name. On the other hand, they inspire the imagination, and they're

not doing any harm. I think we're going to
155 experience cow fatigue and it's going to die out. So we elite in the art world don't have to worry about it too much." Finkelpearl knows whereof[5] he speaks. Some time ago, his then-11-year-old son asked for a miniature replica of
160 one of the entries from CowParade New York 2000 that was selling in his own museum gift shop. "My kid has grown up with a steady diet of high art," Finkelpearl said, laughing, "and this is what he wanted."

---

[5] *whereof*: about which

READING COMPREHENSION

Circle the best answer to the questions. Skim the article to help you find the answers.

1. Why is Edward Sozanski concerned about animal art?
   a. He thinks it's the "scourge of Western civilization."
   b. It is unsophisticated, humorous, and short-lived.
   c. It lowers standards for artists and sponsors.
   d. The displays are not popular enough with tourists.

2. According to the article, which is NOT a reason that animal art exhibitions remain popular?
   a. They are fun for visitors to attend.
   b. They are cheap for sponsors.
   c. They raise money for businesses.
   d. They produce artistic masterpieces.

3. Why does Erika Doss object to the animal art?
   a. It is low quality, unsophisticated, and short-lived.
   b. It does not have enough individualized creativity.
   c. Animals are not an appropriate subject for art.
   d. It discourages sponsors from funding good art.

4. What does Tom Finkelpearl think about animal art?
   a. He thinks it is the worst kind of art possible.
   b. He thinks it is the best kind of art possible.
   c. He thinks it has both problems and benefits.
   d. He thinks it will continue for many years.

VOCABULARY ACTIVITIES

Word Form Chart			
Noun	Verb	Adjective	Adverb
inspector inspection	inspect	....	....
....	....	mutual	mutually
rationalization	rationalize	rational irrational	rationally
legislator legislation legislature	legislate	legislative	....
ethnicity	....	ethnic	ethnically

A. Fill in the blanks with a target word from the chart in the correct form. Use your dictionary to help understand new words. Compare answers with a partner.

1. There has been a big increase in the amount of graffiti on public buildings lately. In fact, the state .... is considering a law making it a crime to paint on buildings.

2. However, local artists are concerned this law will affect public art, which they argue is .... beneficial. The city gets an increase in tourism, and artists get some attention that can lead to more commissions later.

3. The artists .... public art displays by arguing that any exposure to art is a positive thing.

4. The artists' group recognizes that some forms of public art, especially graffiti-style artwork, don't appeal to everyone. Many people see graffiti art as uncontrolled, ... , and silly.

5. However, the artists point to several recently successful pieces of public art, particularly a critically-acclaimed African mural. The bold colors and wild patterns in the mural were .... inspired. The artist's family immigrated here from Kenya and she uses a lot of cultural images in her work.

6. At first, the mural looked like a thick jungle of vines and plants. Upon closer .... , however, you could see human and animal forms moving through the greenery.

7. The artists also argued that the state already has substantial control over public art, since a state engineer must .... every piece of art before it is approved for display.

B. Read these sentences about organizing a public art exhibit. Then, go back and restate each of them in your notebook using the words in parentheses as indicated. Do not change the meanings of the sentences. Discuss your sentences in a small group.

1. Like other kinds of art, public art projects come in many forms, and the resultant aim can be permanent or temporary art. (*goal, ongoing*)

2. Public art can have a sole author with a unique voice, or many participants with multiple viewpoints. (*interpret* or *interpretation*)

3. A good public art project requires the organizers to establish rules that include clearly defined guidelines for reviewing proposals and selecting the project. (*policy, criteria*)

4. A logical evaluation process should be used even if money is being used to create a community-based art project, rather than one done by a paid artist. (*rational, fund* or *funds*)

Rational means "reasonable, sensible, or logical." Likewise, *rationally* means "sensibly or logically." A *rationale* is a reason to do something. These are usually used in positive or unemotional contexts.

> *Decisions about how to use public money must be made **rationally**, with careful consideration given to many criteria.*

The verb *to rationalize* means to "find reasons to explain why you have done something." It is used in situations where there probably is not a good reason, but the person is trying to pretend there is.

> *Although some art experts find animal displays unimpressive, they **rationalize** them by arguing that they increase interest in "real" art.*

C. Read this essay discussing the author's frustration with the public art selection process. In your notebook, summarize the reasons the author gives for his opinion. Use different forms of *rational* in your summary. Discuss your summary in a small group. How many forms of *rational* was your group able to use?

One reason that public art is so terrible is that the entire process is controlled by idiotic bureaucrats and political appointees, many of whom are completely ignorant about art. Because public art offices are part of local government, poor artistic works are often chosen by someone with a low position who justifies his or her choice by saying it was politically necessary.

The selection of projects to receive state funding is done by a committee whose members are rarely selected using sensible criteria. Many members of the committee do not have an ongoing commitment to public art and don't have the education needed to logically consider the merits of different works. Some members do not see the value of "art for art's sake." They give an explanation of their choices based on whether they think the art will help the local economy.

Artists whose pieces are not chosen are often disappointed because they don't understand the reason their work was rejected.

D. Look at these arguments for and against animal art displays like those discussed in this unit. Restate each idea in your notebook, using the word in parentheses. Then, write a paragraph that expresses your own opinion. Try to use as many target words as possible in your work. Be prepared to debate this issue in class.

For	Against
Children, parents, and grandparents can spend quality time at these exhibits, because they can discuss a shared experience. (*mutual*)	Animal parades do not have any of the qualities that are generally used to decide if something should be considered art. (*criteria*)
Displays like Cow Parade have successfully achieved their objective of bringing in shoppers to struggling businesses. (*goal*)	This phenomenon is continuous, with no end in sight, and as more locations follow the trend, the individual identities of the cities are lost. (*ongoing*)
Many young artists see animal art displays as a chance to bring their own ideas and understanding of a theme to a wider audience. (*interpretation, topic*)	Laws that fund public art only allow for a certain amount of money each year, so anything spent on a Cow Parade is taken away from legitimate art. (*legislation*)

E. Self-Assessment Review: Go back to page 33 and reassess your knowledge of the target vocabulary. How has your understanding of the words changed? What words do you feel most comfortable with now?

WRITING AND DISCUSSION TOPICS

1. Some art experts say that art projects do not need to be an installed piece of art. Parades, festivals, and poetry readings can also be considered art. Even public parks, playgrounds, gardens, and buildings can have elements of art. What do you think? Can a parade, for example, be art? Why or why not?

2. Look back at activity C on page 39 and read the material again. Describe a mural that you have seen and feel is interesting or important. What are the proper places for murals? Does public art have to be approved by government to be acceptable? Are big graffiti murals (done without approval) also art? What is their proper place?

3. What are the advantages and disadvantages of having public art with an ethnic focus? Does it bring people together or divide them?

4. Look at the pictures of recent public art pieces on pages 35 and 43. Do you consider the items in these pictures to be art? Is one better than the other? What criteria do you use to decide?

5. Go online and find information about public art in a city not discussed in this unit. Summarize the information and present it to the class. Include your own opinions on whether it really is art and how it benefits or hurts the city.

Unit 4

Public Health

STAYING ALIVE

In this unit, you will

- ➲ read about public health, life expectancy, and the impact of vaccination around the world.
- ➲ read and interpret data in charts, graphs, and tables.
- ➲ increase your understanding of the target academic words for this unit:

approximate	compensate	hierarchy	outcome	resolve
aspect	definite	isolate	radical	straightforward
assure	empirical	layer	recover	

SELF-ASSESSMENT OF TARGET WORDS

Think carefully about how well you know each target word in this unit. Then, write it in the appropriate column in the chart.

I have never seen the word before.	I have seen the word but am not sure what it means.	I understand the word when I see or hear it in a sentence.	I have tried to use the word, but I am not sure I am using it correctly.	I use the word with confidence in either speaking *or* writing.	I use the word with confidence, both in speaking *and* writing.

MORE WORDS YOU'LL NEED

life expectancy: the average number of years a person can expect to live

mortality: the number of deaths in a certain period of time or in a certain place

vaccine: a substance that is given to people to protect them against a particular disease

immunize: to protect someone against a disease by giving a vaccine

immunity: the state of being unaffected by a disease

eradicate: to destroy something (usually a disease) completely

BEFORE YOU READ

A. Answer these questions. Discuss your answers in a small group.

1. Who is the oldest person that you know? How is this person's health?

2. What factors do you think have an impact on life expectancy? Rank these factors from *1* (most important) to *10* (least important).

.... nutrition   .... family history

.... health   .... medical care

.... education   .... geographic location

.... income   .... lifestyle

.... occupation   .... other: ....

3. If you had lived in a different time in history, do you think you would have reached your current age, or would you have died already? Why?

B. This reading contains several graphs and charts. Preview them and predict what the article will be about. Quickly discuss your predictions with a partner.

READ

This article, from the National Bureau of Economic Research in the United States, discusses the factors that affect life expectancy.

The Determinants of Mortality

For most of human history, life expectancy has been short—**approximately** 25 years for our ancient ancestors, and only 37 years for residents of England in 1700. In just the past century,
5 however, life expectancy has increased by over 30 years.

Dramatic changes began in the 18th century. Life expectancy in England rose to 41 years by 1820, 50 years by the early 20th century, and
10 77 years today. A similar shift took place in all developed countries. The drop in mortality rates was particularly **radical** among children (Figure 1). This was because of the near eradication of deaths from infectious diseases—
15 formerly the most common cause of death, since the young are most likely to get infections.

The most important **aspects** of daily life that affected mortality reduction were nutrition, public health measures, and medicine.

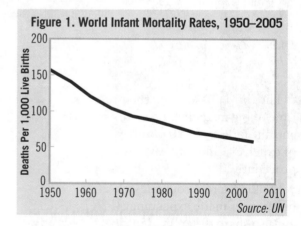

Figure 1. World Infant Mortality Rates, 1950–2005

Source: UN

20 The history of mortality reduction is spoken of in terms of three phases. In the first phase, from the mid-18th century to the mid-19th century, improved nutrition, economic growth, and emerging public health measures played
25 a large role. From the end of the nineteenth century into the twentieth is considered the second phase. Public health became more

important. Because of high mortality rates in cities, urban centers started to deliver clean
30 water (Figure 2) and remove waste. People were also given advice about personal health practices. There was a dramatic reduction in water- and food-borne diseases—typhoid, cholera, dysentery, and tuberculosis. These
35 diseases were practically eradicated in the United States by 1970. By one estimate, water purification alone accounted for half the mortality reduction in the United States in the first third of the twentieth century.

Figure 2. Effect of Filtration and Chlorination on Mortality		
	Total Reduction in Mortality Rate 1900–1936	**Share of Total Due to Clean Water**
Typhoid Mortality	96%	96%*
Total Mortality	30%	43%
Infant Mortality	62%	74%
Child Mortality	81%	62%

Achieved five years after adoption of clean water technologies

40 The third phase, from the 1930s to now, is the time of big medicine. It started with vaccination and antibiotics, and has moved on to a variety of expensive and intensive treatments and procedures.
45 Looking across countries, there are great differences in life expectancy (Figure 3). There are also sharp differences in who dies and from what. Deaths among children account for approximately 30 percent of deaths in poor
50 countries but less than 1 percent of deaths in rich countries. Most deaths in rich countries are from cancers and cardiovascular disease,

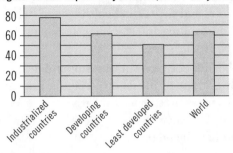

Figure 3. Life Expectancy at Birth, 2001 (in years)

while most deaths in poor countries are from infectious diseases.
55 Though differences persist, many poorer countries have recently experienced large improvements in life expectancy. In India and China, life expectancy has risen by 30 years since 1950. Even in Africa, life expectancy rose by 13
60 years from the early 1950s until the late 1980s, when the spread of HIV/AIDS reversed the trend.
What factors explain this **outcome**? Some of the main factors are changes in income, literacy
65 (especially among women), and the supply of calories. Public health interventions, such as immunization campaigns, improvements in water supply, and the use of antibiotics, have also made a big difference.
70 Although the connection between economic growth and improved health seems **straightforward**, the **empirical** evidence for this is not completely clear. This may be because urbanization[1] often goes along with growth.
75 Growth must be accompanied by effective public health measures in order to bring about mortality reductions.
Within developed countries such as the United States, there are well-documented differences
80 in mortality rates by race, income, education, occupation, or urban/rural status. There is a definite **hierarchy** to healthiness—the higher the socioeconomic status of a group, generally the lower the mortality rate. Some explanations
85 for this include **definite** differences in access to

---

[1] *urbanization*: taking on the characteristics of city life

medical care, in access to the resources needed to buy food and shelter, in health related behaviors such as drinking and smoking, and in levels of "psychosocial stress."

90   The link between social status and health is likely not due to any **isolated** factor. Education, however, seems to have a positive effect on health. This may be due to increased knowledge about health and technology.

95   Is there a universal theory of mortality that can explain improvements over time, differences across countries, and differences across groups? It can be argued that knowledge, science, and technology are important aspects of any logical

100 explanation. As for the future, an increase in the production of new knowledge and treatments is likely to increase inequality in health outcomes in the short term. The silver lining[2], though, is that help is on the way, not only for those who receive

105 it first, but eventually for everyone.

---

[2] *silver lining*: referring to the expression "every cloud has a silver lining," it is the one good aspect of something generally bad

READING COMPREHENSION

Answer the questions in your notebook, looking back at Reading 1 if necessary. Then, compare your answers with a partner.

1. What has happened to life expectancy in the past 30 years?

....

2. Which age group was affected the most? Why?

....

3. What major changes occurred during these time periods?

mid-18th to mid-19th century	
end of 19th to early 20th century	
mid-20th century to now	

4. According to Reading 1, which of these factors positively affect life expectancy? Put a check (✓) next to them. Be prepared to explain your choices.

.... infectious diseases   .... warm climate

.... better nutrition   .... intense medical treatments

.... young parents   .... living in a city

.... many doctors in the community   .... antibiotics

.... clean water   .... lower socioeconomic status

5. What does the article predict for the future of health outcomes?

....

....

READING STRATEGY: Reading and Interpreting Charts, Graphs, and Tables

Charts, graphs, and tables provide vital information and support the information in a text. By presenting information graphically, the reader can see trends and patterns more easily.

People often refer to graphic information as *charts*, regardless of their actual type (chart, graph, table, etc). In academic texts, however, graphic information is usually cited as a *figure*, as in Reading 1. Sometimes, an author will cite figures and tables separately.

A. Match the chart from Reading 1 with its topic.

.... **1.** Figure 1   **a.** effects of water purification

.... **2.** Figure 2   **b.** life expectancy at birth

.... **3.** Figure 3   **c.** world infant mortality rates

B. With a partner, discuss the charts in Reading 1 by answering these questions.

Figure 1: What general trend can you see? What do you expect to happen in the future, based on this information?

Figure 2: What percentage of reduction in infant mortality is a result of clean water? What conclusions can you draw about clean water and mortality rate?

Figure 3: Which region has the lowest life expectancy at birth? Which region has the highest? What is surprising or interesting to you in this chart? Based on this chart, how long can you expect to live? Do you agree with the prediction? Why or why not?

STEP I VOCABULARY ACTIVITIES: Word Level

A. Scan Reading 1 for these target vocabulary words and match them with their definitions. Use a dictionary to help you.

.... **1.** radical   **a.** an end result; consequence

.... **2.** aspect   **b.** based on experiments or practical experience, not ideas

.... **3.** approximately   **c.** very great, extreme

.... **4.** outcome   **d.** certain, without doubt

.... **5.** straightforward   **e.** not quite exact or correct

.... **6.** empirical   **f.** solitary; alone

.... **7.** definite   **g.** a distinct feature or element

.... **8.** isolated   **h.** easy to understand, simple

The words *radical* (adjective) and *radically* (adverb) are used to describe changes in something. The noun *radical* means "a person who wants great social or political changes."

B. Complete these sentences with the correct form of *radical*.

1. There were .... changes in life expectancy with the introduction of clean water.

2. The life expectancy of infants changed .... with the use of vaccinations.

3. In the early days of vaccination, some doctors were considered .... for supporting the idea of mass immunization.

4. The aspect of public health that has most .... affected people's lives is clean water.

5. The spread of HIV/AIDS has made a .... difference in public health policy around the world.

The word *aspect* refers to one of the qualities or parts of a situation, idea, or problem. It takes the preposition *of*.

*One **aspect** of a person's socioeconomic status is income level.*

C. What are some aspects of these situations that a person should consider before making a decision?

1. deciding which college to attend
2. deciding on a career path
3. choosing a movie to watch with a friend
4. choosing a movie to watch with your mother
5. making vacation plans
6. renting an apartment

STEP II VOCABULARY ACTIVITIES: Sentence Level

D. Which of these things is straightforward? Do any of them have aspects that are straightforward but are not straightforward as a whole? Discuss your answers in a small group. Give examples to support your ideas.

1. buying a used car
2. communication with your boss
3. going to the doctor
4. picking up a package
5. doing homework
6. trading music with a friend

Word Form Chart

Noun	Verb	Adjective	Adverb
approximation	approximate	approximate	approximately
definiteness	....	definite	definitely
isolation	isolate	isolated	....

E. Read the information about the effects of clean water on public health. Then go back and restate each sentence using the word in parentheses. Discuss your sentences with a partner or in a small group.

1. At the start of the 20th century, high mortality rates were common in America, specifically in urban areas. Yet by 1940, these rates had dropped, with life expectancy rising from 47 to 63 years. (*isolated, definite*)

   *Early in the 20th century, high mortality rates were somewhat **isolated** in urban America, but by 1940 there was a **definite** drop and people lived much longer.*

2. The introduction of water filtration and chlorination in major U.S. cities accounted for roughly half of the 30 percent decline in urban death rates during 1900–1940. (*approximately* or *approximate*)

3. Clean water was, without a doubt, one of the most significant causes of rapid health improvements in the nation's history. (*definitely*)

4. Researchers began focusing on the role of clean water alone, after they discovered that deaths dropped sharply in cities that filtered their drinking water. (*isolate* or *isolated*)

F. Rewrite this sentence two ways, using the form of *approximate* indicated.

   Clean water was responsible for cutting about three-quarters of deaths and nearly two-thirds of child mortality in the United States in the first 40 years of the 20th century.

1. approximate (*adjective*)

   ....

   ....

   ....

   ....

2. approximately

   ....

   ....

   ....

   ....

> A *hierarchy* is "a system of organization that has many grades or ranks from the lowest to the highest." The adjective form is *hierarchical*.
>
> *I prefer to work in a cooperative setting, with people at my level. I don't want to be in a **hierarchical** environment with lots of bosses.*

G. What do you think is the hierarchy in each of these situations? Rank the people from most important (1) to least important (5) in each case. Discuss your hierarchies in a small group. In what other situations have you noticed hierarchies?

a. School

.... teacher

.... principal/director

.... older students

.... my class

.... new students

b. Health center

.... doctor

.... nurse

.... patient

.... technicians

.... clerks

c. Family

.... mother

.... me

.... grandparents

.... siblings

.... father

READING 2

BEFORE YOU READ

A. Read these questions. Discuss your answers in a small group.

1. What are some common childhood diseases? Did you have any of them?

2. Do you know which vaccines you received as a child? If so, what were they for? How were they delivered (by mouth, by injection, etc.)? If you remember the experience, what was it like? Were you scared? Did it hurt?

3. Imagine that a drug company develops a vaccine that it says will protect against all major diseases. They need volunteers to test the vaccine. Would you volunteer? Why or why not?

B. Preview the tables in Reading 2. What do you think this text will discuss? Compare your ideas with a partner.

Immunization against Diseases of Public Health Importance

The benefits of immunization

Vaccines—which protect against disease by **assuring** immunity—are widely and routinely given around the world. This practice is based
5 on the idea that it is better to ke ep people from falling ill than to focus only on helping them **recover** once they are ill. Suffering, disability, and death are avoided. Immunization prevented about two million deaths in 2002. In addition,
10 infection is reduced, strain on health-care systems is eased, and money is frequently saved that can be used for other health services.

Immunization is a proven tool for controlling and even eradicating disease. An immunization
15 campaign carried out by the World Health Organization (WHO) from 1967 to 1977 eradicated the natural occurrence of smallpox. When the program began, the disease still threatened 60% of the world's population
20 and killed every fourth victim. Eradication of poliomyelitis is within reach. Since the launch by WHO and its partners of the Global Polio Eradication Initiative in 1988, infections have fallen by 99%, and about five million people
25 have escaped paralysis. Between 1999 and 2003, measles deaths dropped worldwide by almost 40%, and some regions have **resolved** to eliminate the disease.

Global immunization coverage

30 Coverage has greatly increased since WHO's Expanded Program on Immunization began in 1974, and the results are encouraging (Table 1). In 2003, global DTP3 (three doses of the diphtheria-tetanus-pertussis combination
35 vaccine) coverage was 78%—up from 20% in

Table 1. Annual deaths* in 2002 from vaccine-preventable diseases

Disease	Under 5	Over 5	Total
Diphtheria	4 000	1 000	5 000
Measles	540 000	70 000	610 000
Polio	-----	-----	1 000
Tetanus	198 000	15 000	213 000
Pertussis	294 000	-----	294 000
Hepatitis B	-----	600 000	600 000
Haemophilus influenzae b (Hib)	386 000	-----	386 000
Yellow fever	15 000	15 000	30 000
TOTAL	**1 437 000**	**701 000**	**2 138 000**

* *WHO Estimates (January 2005)*

1980. However, 27 million children worldwide were not reached by DTP3 in 2003, including 9.9 million in South Asia and 9.6 million in sub-Saharan Africa.

40 ## Vaccines under development

Numerous new vaccines with major potential for improving health in developing countries are in research and development (Table 2). They include vaccines for rotavirus diarrhea, which

Table 2. Annual deaths in 2002 from diseases for which vaccines will be available soon

Disease	Under 5	Over 5	Total
Meningitis AC*	10 000	16 000	26 000
Rotavirus*	402 000	47 000	449 000
Pneumococcal Disease*	716 000	897 000	1 612 000
TOTAL	**1 128 000**	**960 000**	**2 087 000**

* *WHO Estimates (January 2005)*

kills 300,000 to 600,000 children under age five every year. Several of these vaccines may be available in developing countries by 2008–2009.

History

Introducing a small amount of smallpox virus by inhaling through the nose or by making a number of small pricks through the **layers** of skin (variolation) to create resistance to the disease began in the 10th or 11th century in Central Asia. Variolation was introduced into England in 1721. There, in 1798, Edward Jenner began treatments against smallpox, the first systematic effort to control a disease through immunization.

In 1885, Louis Pasteur developed the first vaccine to protect humans against rabies. Vaccines against diphtheria and tetanus were introduced in the early 1900s, the Calmette-Guérin vaccine (against tuberculosis) in 1927, the Salk polio vaccine in 1955, and vaccines against measles and mumps in the 1960s.

How vaccines work

Vaccines typically provide the immune system with harmless copies of an *antigen*: a portion of the surface of a bacterium or virus that the immune system recognizes as "foreign." A vaccine may also provide a non-active version of a toxin— a poison produced by a bacterium—so that the body can create a defense against it.

Once an antigen is noticed by the immune system, white blood cells called B-lymphocytes create a protein called an antibody that is designed to attach to that antigen. Many copies of this antibody are produced. If a true infection of the same disease occurs, still more antibodies are created, and as they attach to their targets they may block the activity of the virus or bacterial strain directly, thus fighting infection. In addition, once in place, the antibodies make it much easier for other parts of the immune system to recognize and destroy the invading agent.

Immune systems are designed to "remember." Once exposed to a particular bacterium or virus, they retain immunity against it for years, decades, or even a lifetime. This means they are prepared to quickly defeat a later infection. This is a huge benefit because a body encountering a germ for the first time may need from seven to 12 days to effectively defend it, and by then serious illness and even death may occur.

Effectiveness and safety

All vaccines used for routine immunization are very effective in preventing disease, although no vaccine attains 100% effectiveness. More than one dose of a vaccine is generally given to increase the chance of developing immunity.

Vaccines are very safe, and side effects are minor—especially when compared with the diseases they are designed to prevent. Serious complications occur rarely. For example, severe allergic reactions result at a rate of one for every 100,000 doses of measles vaccine. Two to four cases of vaccine-associated paralytic polio have been reported for every one million children receiving oral polio vaccine.

The cost-effectiveness of immunization

Immunization is considered among the most cost-effective of health investments. There is a well-defined target group; contact with the health system is only needed at the time of delivery; and vaccination does not require any major change of lifestyle.

A recent study estimated that a one-week "supplemental immunization activity" against measles carried out in Kenya in 2002—in which 12.8 million children were vaccinated—would result in a net saving in health costs of US$12 million over the following ten years; during that time it would prevent 3,850,000 cases of measles and 125,000 deaths. The cost of the immunizations is clearly **compensated** for by its life-saving value.

READING COMPREHENSION

A. Mark each sentence as *T* (true) or *F* (false) according to the information in Reading 2.

.... 1. Vaccines protect against suffering, disability, and death.

.... 2. Smallpox has been eradicated through immunization.

.... 3. Variolation first began in West Africa.

.... 4. The first vaccine was developed to protect humans against rabies.

.... 5. There is no problem reaching all of the children worldwide with immunizations.

.... 6. Once immune systems are exposed to a bacterium or virus, they "remember" it and can easily fight against an infection later.

.... 7. Side effects and serious complications from vaccines occur frequently.

.... 8. Immunization is extremely expensive and many question whether it is cost-effective.

B. Use the tables in Reading 2 to complete these sentences. Compare your answers with a partner.

1. .... deaths were caused by polio in 2002.

2. The disease .... caused the same number of deaths in people under 5 and over 5 in 2002.

3. .... caused the most total deaths in 2002.

4. .... killed more people over 5 years old than small children.

5. .... deaths from meningitis in 2002 could have been prevented if there was a vaccine.

6. A vaccine for rotavirus will have the most effect on people who are ....

READING STRATEGY

Another type of chart is called a pie chart. It is used to show how one thing or group of things is divided.

A. Study this example of a pie chart and answer the questions below.

Vaccine-Preventable Diseases

In 2002, WHO estimated that 1.4 million deaths among children under 5 years were due to diseases that could have been prevented by routine vaccination.

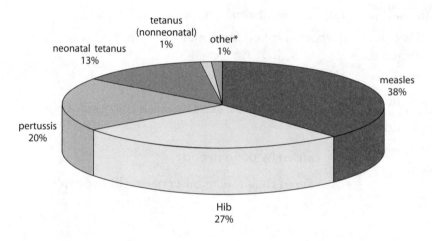

* other - polio, diphtheria, yellow fever

1. What percentage of children who died from preventable diseases died from Hib?

....

2. What was the most common preventable disease that killed children?

....

3. How many actual deaths were caused by "other" diseases? ....

B. Read this paragraph about the polio vaccine. Then, in your notebook, create a chart, graph, table, or pie chart depicting some or all of the information. Discuss your chart in a small group.

The discovery and use of polio vaccines has all but eliminated polio in the Americas. In 1960, there were 2,525 cases of paralytic polio in the United States. By 1965, there were 61. Between 1980 and 1990, cases averaged 8 per year, and most of those were induced by vaccination. There has not been a single case of polio caused by the wild virus since 1979. In 1994, polio was declared eradicated in all of the Americas. In 1988, the World Health Organization set a goal of eradication of polio from the entire world by the year 2000.

STEP I VOCABULARY ACTIVITIES: Word Level

A. Read these facts about the eradication of smallpox. Then, complete the sentences using the target vocabulary in the box.

approximately	isolated	radical
assured	layers	recovered
definite	outcome	resolved

1. During the 15th century, an early form of smallpox vaccination was practiced in China and other parts of the world. Healthy people were intentionally infected through the .... of skin with substances from the pustules of people suffering from smallpox.

2. Later, in the 18th century, this practice was adopted in England, where smallpox was the most common disease, causing .... 20% of all deaths in London. An expression of the times was, "Mothers counted their children only after they had had the smallpox."

3. An English doctor, Edward Jenner, created the first vaccine in 1796. Dr. Jenner had heard that dairymaids, ... from other people in the countryside, often had cowpox, a milder disease related to smallpox.

4. After the dairymaids .... from cowpox, they were immune to smallpox. Jenner .... to find out why.

5. Jenner performed the first vaccination on a boy with material taken from lesions of cowpox. The .... was that the boy, and all people who received the vaccine later, were immune to smallpox.

6. In the 19th century, vaccination laws were established in Europe and the United States. These laws .... people that vaccination was safe, and they began to be vaccinated against smallpox routinely. In the 20th century, vaccination against smallpox became a worldwide effort.

7. The last .... case of smallpox in the United States was reported in 1949, and routine vaccination of children in the United States ended in 1971. The last case of smallpox in the world was in Ethiopia in 1976.

8. In 1980, scientists announced that the once .... idea of vaccines had been successful at eradicating smallpox from the world.

To *assure* means to promise somebody something will certainly happen or will be true, especially if he/she is worried.

*The doctor **assured** us this vaccination is perfectly safe.*

B. What might each of these people want to *assure* someone of? Discuss your ideas in a small group.

1. a teenager to a parent
2. a student to a teacher
3. a friend to another friend
4. a husband to a wife
5. an employer to an employee

STEP II VOCABULARY ACTIVITIES: Sentence Level

The verb *resolve* has two definitions. It can mean "to find a solution to a problem" or "to decide something and be determined not to change your mind."

*Most of the difficulties have been **resolved**.*

*Ray **resolved** never to let that same thing happen again.*

The noun *resolve* means "a strong determination to achieve something."

*The difficulties in her way merely strengthened her **resolve**.*

There is another noun form as well. *Resolution* is more formal and refers to a firm decision to do or not to do something.

*The United Nations made a **resolution** to eradicate polio around the world.*

C. Read these reasons why immunization is a cost-effective public health policy. Restate each one using a form of the word *resolve*. Be prepared to read aloud or discuss your sentences in a small group or with the class.

1. By preventing disease, immunization allows countries to reduce the amount of money spent on treatment and hospitalization costs.

   If countries resolve to prevent disease through immunization, less money will be used on medical treatment or hospitalization.

2. Immunization helps national governments avoid the expense of treating major outbreaks of disease and the loss of productivity that comes with these illnesses.

3. Immunization also increases productivity by allowing parents to work instead of staying home to care for sick children.

4. It costs just $17 to immunize a child with the six core vaccines: polio, diphtheria, pertussis, measles, tetanus, and tuberculosis.

5. Most immunizations cost less than $50 per healthy life year saved.

D. Review each section of Reading 2. Write 2–3 sentences in your notebook that summarize the main idea of each section. Use the target vocabulary in parentheses in your summaries.

1. the benefits of immunization (*assure, resolve*)
2. global immunization coverage (*definite*)
3. vaccines under development (*approximate*)
4. history (*layers*)
5. how vaccines work (*recover*)
6. effectiveness and safety (*aspect*)
7. the cost-effectiveness of immunization (*compensate*)

To *compensate* means "to remove or reduce the bad effect of something" or "to make up for something."

*He **compensated** for his lack of money by doing most of the work himself.*

As a noun, *compensation* can refer to the money that you pay to somebody or to something that removes or reduced the bad effect of something.

*Some companies provide a shuttle bus to the nearest train station as part of their **compensation** to employees.*

*The owner of the property had to pay **compensation** to the woman who slipped on his stairs and broke her leg.*

E. What sort of compensation (if any) should the people get in each situation? Discuss your ideas in a small group. Then, choose one situation and write a paragraph explaining your opinion. Be prepared to read your work aloud to the class.

1. Your son is riding his bicycle in a city park. He loses control for a moment and goes onto the grass. He hits a hole in the ground and is thrown from his bike, breaking his arm and ruining the bike.
2. Your girlfriend or boyfriend has bought tickets to a sold-out concert of your favorite band. You decide to take a nap before the show but sleep too long. The concert is half over by the time you wake up.
3. Your family is moving to a new apartment and there is a lot of mess and confusion. Your parents are stressed out and very busy. So busy, in fact, that they have clearly forgotten that today is your birthday.

F. Self-Assessment Review: Go back to page 49 and reassess your knowledge of the target vocabulary. How has your understanding of the words changed? What words do you feel most comfortable with now?

WRITING AND DISCUSSION TOPICS

1. Go online and research some of the arguments against immunization. Summarize them and give your own opinion on the subject.

2. Some important aspects of life expectancy include lifestyle choices (such as drinking, smoking, and overall health behavior), education, family history, and nutrition. Are there other contributing factors that were not discussed in the unit? What are they? Why are they significant?

3. It has been argued that clean water has had the single most important impact in public health and the eradication of disease. What do you predict will be the next great step in public health or the next great medical discovery?

4. Diseases like smallpox have been eradicated, and common viruses that cause the flu have been controlled, but there is still the possibility a deadly disease or virus could occur in our lifetime. What can governments do to prepare for such a global health risk?

BODIES IN MOTION

In this unit, you will

- ⊃ read about the latest developments in photographic motion studies conducted for science, industry, medicine, athletics, and art.
- ⊃ practice summarizing a text, including any accompanying images.
- ⊃ increase your understanding of the target academic words for this unit:

abstract	display	expose	restore	transit
appreciate	drama	hence	sequence	version
available	encounter	image	series	visible

SELF-ASSESSMENT OF TARGET WORDS

Think carefully about how well you know each target word in this unit. Then, write it in the appropriate column in the chart.

I have never seen the word before.	I have seen the word but am not sure what it means.	I understand the word when I see or hear it in a sentence.	I have tried to use the word, but I am not sure I am using it correctly.	I use the word with confidence in either speaking *or* writing.	I use the word with confidence, both in speaking *and* writing.

BEFORE YOU READ

Read these questions. Discuss your answers in a small group.

1. How do you assess your own performance in sports, or another physical activity (dance, aerobics, etc.)?

2. Do you like the slow-motion replays of important moments in a sports program? Why or why not? What is the point of them?

3. Have you ever seen video of your performance? If so, was it helpful? How? If not, do you think it would be helpful? How?

READ

The first selection was adapted from the "Collision Detection" column of the online magazine *Slate*. The second selection was adapted from press releases by BBC Sport.

The Dartfish Olympics

Posted by: Clive Thompson,
August 24, 10:55 AM

If you've watched the most recent summer and winter Olympics, you've probably seen StroMotion—the photo software that breaks an athlete's fluid movements into stop-motion-
5 style freeze-frames. This very cool software is made by the Swiss company Dartfish, and apparently Olympians have been using it to train in an incredibly innovative way. They use film footage of the performance of a past Olympic
10 athlete and **display** it alongside footage of themselves. Both sequences are broken down into StroMotion frames.

As the Associated Press reports, U.S. pole vault star Toby Stevenson uses Dartfish to
15 virtually "compete against" a video of Sergey Bubka, the world record holder.

"I use it until smoke comes out of the machine. It's great," said Stevenson, who has secured a spot on the Olympic team. Stevenson
20 can review his practice jumps on a laptop within seconds. Within two hours of a track meet, he can watch himself on an LCD projector back at the hotel. Or he can have his day's work burned onto a CD.

25 While Stevenson's muscles tell him one thing, the digital video might display something else. "It's a big reason for my success," Stevenson said. "I jump, and between every jump I watch my jump, and after practice I watch every jump on
30 Dartfish."

An example of StroMotion technology

This reminds me of the idea of the "ghost" competition in many popular video games. I first **encountered** it in the original Mario Kart back in 1996: You could race around a track and
35 then do it again, competing against a recorded, "ghost," **version** of yourself. Competing against your ghost—or that of a world-ranked competitor—is now a pretty common thing in many games. It reminds me of how game
40 innovations have constantly pioneered techniques that are transforming how we view, and play, real-world sports.

There is some debate about whether this is a good thing. Some famous judges—such as
45 Cynthia Potter, NBC's famous diving analyst— wonder whether StroMotion is harming the sport. When judges use it, it might encourage them to give demerits[1] for things they normally wouldn't see. As *USA Today* reports, "With the
50 naked eye, you don't see these tiny little things that might be called deductions," said Potter, as divers lined up for midday practice plunges[2] at the Olympic venue. "I don't know if you'd even need judges if you could program all this into a
55 computer."

But, she says, "Human judges allow for artistic judgment—and allow divers to put personality in their dives."

Of course, this isn't an entirely new thing.
60 The photo finish has been around for decades in many sports—and has caused huge controversies in everything from the 100-meter dash to greyhound racing. Modern media are likely to make things even stranger. I can easily envision
65 the next few Olympics, when fans are getting personalized StroMotion streams sent to their mobile phones, which they can view and then vote on which athlete did the best dive.

---

[1] *demerit*: a point against something that is being judged
[2] *plunge*: a sudden, forceful fall or dive into something
[3] *trajectory*: the path of something in motion
[4] *half-pipe*: a U-shaped, high-sided ramp
[5] *spontaneity*: unplanned action arising from a momentary impulse

BBC Sport Uses StroMotion Technique

70 BBC Sport is a leader in sports broadcasting innovation and was the first network in British television to use the StroMotion technique.

StroMotion is an **image** enhancement technique. It creates stunning video footage
75 displaying the evolution of an athlete's movement, technique, execution, and tactics over space and time.

Television sports viewers are able to see an athletic movement, such as the line of a skier,
80 unfold before their eyes by compounding video images into a frame-by-frame **sequence**. The StroMotion concept is based on stroboscoping, a means to analyze rapid movement so that a moving object is perceived as a **series** of static
85 images along the object's trajectory[3].

StroMotion special effects add particular value to winter sports. For example, the StroMotion technique applied to an ice skater during a jump allows us to clearly see the technique and
90 quality of its execution by highlighting the maneuver—the preparation phase, the elevation progression, the inclination and straightness of the body, and the quality and speed of execution.

Applied to the half-pipe[4] events in gravity-
95 extreme sports such as snowboarding, skateboarding, and skiing, StroMotion allows viewers to fully appreciate the technique and the quality of aerial maneuvers (spontaneity[5], elevation, landing) and highlights the different
100 phases and their **transitions**.

Roger Mosey, BBC Sport Director, said, "Innovation is very important to us in BBC Sport, and our coverage of the Olympics will continue to showcase both new technology in
105 the coverage and greater choice of coverage for people with access to digital services."

The StroMotion technology is worldwide patent-protected and is exclusively **available** from Dartfish products and services.

READING COMPREHENSION

Mark each sentence as *T* (true) or *F* (false) according to the information in Reading 1. Correct each false statement on the line below it.

.... **1.** Using StroMotion, it's possible for an Olympic athlete to observe his or her technique and compare it with that of a champion from the past.

....

.... **2.** The Olympic athlete Toby Stevenson sometimes feels he has made a good jump, but the StroMotion doesn't always confirm this.

....

.... **3.** Some diving analysts don't like StroMotion replays because they don't take into account a diver's creativity and artistry.

....

.... **4.** StroMotion is the first photographic technique to cause controversy in sports.

....

.... **5.** Clive Thompson predicts that the viewers themselves might soon be voting on Olympic dives after watching them on their cell phones.

....

.... **6.** StroMotion would probably be useful in viewing any sport that involves jumping.

....

.... **7.** StroMotion is of no value in viewing summer sports.

....

.... **8.** Many different companies sell StroMotion technology.

....

READING STRATEGY: Summarize a Text, Including Nontext Elements

> The task of summarizing a text can be broken down into two steps:
> - Figure out the central ideas of a selection.
> - Combine them briefly and clearly.
>
> Also be sure to include the nontext elements—such as pictures, tables, charts, and graphs—in your summary.

1. Identify two main ideas in *The Dartfish Olympics*.

   ....

   ....

2. Identify two main ideas in *BBC Sport Uses StroMotion Technique*.

   ....

   ....

3. Look at the photo that accompanies the reading selection. How does it link to the main ideas? Consider the photo on its own. What main idea does it present?

   ....

   ....

4. Combine the main ideas from 1, 2, and 3 above into a summary of Reading 1. One or two sentences should be enough.

   ....

   ....

STEP I VOCABULARY ACTIVITIES: Word Level

A. Put each word in the box in the correct column, based on which target word it is a synonym for. Use your dictionary to check the meanings of new words.

accessible	obtainable	understand
advertised	show	usable
exhibit	treasure	value

available	**display**	**appreciate**
....	....	....
....	....	....
....	....	....

Word Form Chart

Noun	Verb	Adjective	Adverb
appreciation	appreciate	appreciative appreciated unappreciated	appreciatively

Appreciate, as a transitive verb, takes an object and means

    to value   *The ex-prisoners **appreciated** their freedom.*

    to be thankful for   *We really **appreciated** his help.*

    to understand the   *I can **appreciate** why this is such*
    significance of something   *a big problem for you.*

Note: As an intransitive verb, *appreciate* does not take an object and means "to increase in value over time." It is a very common word in business and art. The opposite is *depreciate*.

    *The property they bought last year has already **appreciated** 25%.*

    *The value of a new car **depreciates** as soon as you buy it.*

B. Complete the sentences with the correct form of *appreciate* from the chart above.

1. Her favorite courses in high school were in art and music ....

2. My friend was very .... when we gave him a going-away party.

3. His art collection .... greatly over a period of forty years.

4. Their gift to us was very thoughtful and much ....

5. Because they are so rare, the old coins have .... in value.

C. Which of these things do you value most? Rank them from *1* (most appreciated) to *6* (least appreciated). Discuss your choices with a partner.

.... your mother's advice   .... your cell phone

.... quiet neighbors   .... air conditioning

.... mass transit   .... privacy

D. Which of these things does an adult appreciate better than a child? Write *A* for things adults appreciate, *C* for things children better appreciate, or *B* for things both groups can appreciate equally. Discuss your choices with a partner.

.... the value of sleep .... the taste of chocolate

.... the importance of family .... a surprise birthday party

.... a good joke .... kindness

STEP II VOCABULARY ACTIVITIES: Sentence Level

An *image* has both concrete and abstract meanings, but they all connect to the idea of a picture of something.

*The **images** on the screen reminded him of the town where he grew up.*

*The **image** of the building was beautifully reflected in the lake.*

*Many people have the **image** of Canada as being cold all the time.*

*Ads try to create a positive **image** of a product.*

The verb *imagine* and the noun *imagination* also come from the word *image*.

There are many expressions and collocations that feature the word *image*.

She is the very image of her sister.   (She looks exactly like her sister.)

He is the very image of sophistication. (He has all the qualities of sophistication.)

She is the spitting image of her father. (She looks and acts like her father.)

E. Match each use of the word *image* with the field to which it typically belongs. Then, write an example sentence for each context. Discuss your sentences in a small group.

.... **1.** art
a. the public personality or character presented by a person

.... **2.** psychology
b. a symbol or metaphor that represents something else

.... **3.** business/marketing
c. a duplication of the visual form of a person or object

.... **4.** literature
d. an advertising concept conveyed to the public

....

....

....

....

F. The word *version* is very common in the software and publishing industries. Complete the example sentences with the correct term from the box. Then write a new example sentence for each term. Use your dictionary as necessary. Be prepared to read aloud or discuss your new sentences in class.

> **a.** electronic version   **d.** revised version
> **b.** latest version   **e.** standard version
> **c.** original version   **f.** updated version

1. For a home computer, the ......*e*...... of the program is usually good enough.
   The standard version of this program has all the basic tools a student needs.

2. Some of the information in this manual is old. They need to put out an ....

3. I found some earlier drafts of the proposal, but I need to see the .... of it.

4. There were some mistakes in the book, but they were all corrected in the ....

5. You can buy a newspaper at the coffee shop or read the .... online.

6. The remake of that movie was okay, but I prefer the ....

G. Discuss these questions in a small group.

1. Are you the spitting image of someone in your family? Who? In what ways are you like each other?

2. Do you know someone who is the spitting image of someone else? Who?

3. Who or what would you describe as

   the very image of success   the very image of evil
   the very image of beauty   the very image of power
   the very image of elegance   the very image of fun

H. Choose one item from question 3 in activity G and write a paragraph about your choice. Be prepared to read your paragraph aloud and discuss your opinions.

BEFORE YOU READ

Read these questions. Discuss your answers in a small group.

1. When a horse gallops, do you think all four hooves ever leave the ground at the same time? Why or why not?

2. What does a splash look like? Describe a splash of water or a raindrop as it hits the ground. What happens?

3. Have you ever seen an electronic strobe light in action? Where? In what situation or for what function?

Freeze Frames— Stopping Time

For most people, the arc of their golf swing or tennis stroke is an **abstract** image, something that happens much too fast for the unaided eye to see. Fortunately, modern athletes have a
5 special tool available—StroMotion—with which to obtain and study an actual, **visible** record of their movements. But StroMotion is not a brand new concept—in fact it's an old idea newly linked to digital video and computer software.
10 StroMotion uses processes and technology developed by photographic pioneers such as Eadweard Muybridge, who conducted the first photographic sequential motion studies, and Harold Edgerton, inventor of the strobe
15 light, which seems to stop even the speediest objects—like bullets—in transit.

In 1872, Leland Stanford—the soon-to-be Governor of California who was also a businessman, horse lover, racetrack owner,
20 and later founder of Stanford University— encountered this commonly debated question of the time: whether during a horse's gallop all four hooves were ever off the ground at the same time. This was called "unsupported transit,"
25 and Stanford took it upon himself to settle this popular debate scientifically. He hired a well-known British photographer named Eadweard Muybridge, then working in San Francisco, to get the answer.

30 By 1878, Muybridge had successfully photographed a horse in fast motion using a series of fifty cameras. The cameras were arranged along a track parallel to the horse's, and each of the camera shutters was triggered by
35 electronic timers developed specifically for the project. The resulting series of photos proved that the hooves do all leave the ground at the same time—although not with the legs fully extended forward and back, as artists of the day
40 had imagined, but rather at the moment when all the hooves are tucked under the horse, as it switches from "pulling" from the front legs to "pushing" from the back legs.

Muybridge continued to use this technique
45 to photograph human beings and animals in order to "freeze" and study their motion. He made sequential motion studies of athletes in a wide variety of sports and additional studies of everyday people performing
50 mundane movements like walking down stairs. Muybridge's work helped inaugurate the modern science of biomechanics, the research and analysis of the mechanics of living organisms.

Furthermore, when a viewer flips rapidly
55 through a sequence of Muybridge's pictures, it appears to the eye that the original motion

Muybridge's *The Horse in Motion*

has been **restored**. Viewers **appreciated** these images for reasons of both science and entertainment, and inventors like Thomas
60 Edison were inspired to work harder on the creation of a motion picture process. **Hence** Muybridge is considered to have been a crucial figure in the development of movies.

Muybridge showed that the value of a
65 sequence of photographs could be greater than that of any single image, a lesson that was later applied in photojournalism as well as biomechanics. But after Muybridge, inventors persisted in seeking ways to photograph faster
70 and faster motion, and eventually they came back to the stroboscope.

A stroboscope, also known as a strobe, is an instrument used to make a fast-moving object appear to be slow-moving or stationary[1]. It is
75 mainly employed in industry for the study of the motion of objects, such as rotating machine parts or vibrating strings.

The stroboscope was designed by Joseph Plateau of Belgium in 1832. In its simplest form,
80 it is a rotating disc with evenly-spaced small openings cut into it. It is placed between the observer and the moving object and rotates to alternately block and reveal the object. When the speed of the disc is adjusted so that
85 it becomes synchronized[2] with the object's movement, the object seems to slow and stop. The illusion is commonly known as the "stroboscopic effect."

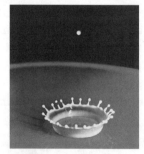

Milkdrop Coronet, 1957

---

[1] *stationary*: still, not moving
[2] *synchronized*: matching, in step with

In 1931, almost exactly one hundred years
90 after Plateau, an engineering professor at the Massachusetts Institute of Technology named Harold Edgerton combined the stroboscope and the camera. He created an electronic version of the strobe in which the rotating disc was
95 replaced by a special lamp. The lamp emits brief and rapid flashes of light. The frequency of the flash is adjusted so that it is a fraction of the object's speed. At this point, the object appears to be stationary.

100 Although his original goal was to display and study the stresses on moving machine parts otherwise invisible to the naked eye, Edgerton later used very short flashes of light as a means of producing **dramatic** still photographs of
105 fast-moving objects in transit, such as bullets in flight, hovering hummingbirds, and falling milk drops splashing into a bowl. His camera had no shutter. The film was pulled through continuously as in motion picture cameras—but
110 at much higher speeds—and **exposed** by a stroboscopic flash lasting 1/1,000,000 of a second or less.

Edgerton's invention was the basis for the built-in light flash found in nearly all cameras
115 today. Strobes are also popular as a lighting effect in nightclubs, where they create the appearance of dancing in slow motion. Other common uses are in alarm systems, theatrical lighting (for example, to simulate lightning), and
120 as high-visibility navigation lights.

In medicine, stroboscopes are used to view the vocal cords. Both the strobe and the camera are placed inside the patient's neck using a procedure called endoscopy. The patient then
125 hums or speaks into a microphone, which in turn activates the stroboscope. Doctors can see the movement of the vocal chords and diagnose problems.

Strobe technology has also been instrumental
130 in the development of underwater scanning technology—useful in searching the sea

bottom for shipwrecks—and is valuable in photographing creatures living in the darkest depths of the ocean. Edgerton worked with the undersea explorer Jacques Cousteau, providing him with underwater stroboscopes.

In addition to having the science, engineering, and business skills to advance strobe lighting commercially, Edgerton is equally appreciated for his visual flair. Many of the dramatic images he created for science are now found in art museums worldwide. In Edgerton's strobe work, science and art encounter one another and find that in some way they serve the same need for exactitude—a goal shared by the athletes who use video StroMotion today to improve their competitive performance.

READING COMPREHENSION

Mark each sentence as *T* (true) or *F* (false) according to the information in Reading 1. Correct each false statement on the line below it.

.... 1. Stanford hired Muybridge to find out whether both wings flap simultaneously when a chicken is flying, but Muybridge switched to studying horses.

....

.... 2. Muybridge failed to prove conclusively that all four of a horse's hooves do at some point leave the ground at the same time.

....

.... 3. Before Muybridge made his motion studies, painters had incorrectly portrayed a horse's gallop.

....

.... 4. Motion picture inventor Thomas Edison was aware of Muybridge's work.

....

.... 5. Edgerton's electronic strobe light and the built-in flash units in today's cameras are unrelated inventions.

....

.... 6. Creatures living in the darkest depths of the sea were made visible by Edgerton's strobes.

....

.... 7. The need for exactness is common to art, science, and athletics.

....

.... 8. Photographs can expand our world by showing us things we can't normally see.

....

READING STRATEGY

1. Identify two main topics in Reading 2.

   ....

   ....

2. Look at the photos that accompany Reading 2. How do they link to the main ideas? Consider the photos as a group. What main idea does the group present?

   ....

   ....

3. Combine the main ideas from the text and the accompanying images into a summary of Reading 2.

   ....

   ....

   ....

   ....

STEP I VOCABULARY ACTIVITIES: Word Level

A. Complete these sentences using the target vocabulary in the box.

abstract	dramatist	transition	visibility
dramatic	invisible	transitional	

1. Many believe that the best .... in English was Shakespeare. He wrote at least 37 plays.

2. When writing an essay, it is important to use a .... to connect the ideas in one paragraph with those in the next paragraph.

3. A painting without a story or representational image is referred to as .... art.

4. The observation deck at the top of a tall building provides the best view of a city, but only if there is clear .... that day.

5. The strong contrast between light and dark in black-and-white films can create quite a .... effect.

6. Magicians can use strobes and other lighting tricks to make objects seem .... , even though they are actually right in front of you.

7. The office hasn't moved completely to the new location yet. We're still in a .... phase.

B. Put each word in the box in the correct column, based on which target word it is a synonym for. Use your dictionary to check the meanings of new words.

bring back	reveal	therefore
consequently	revive	thus
renovate	show	uncover

expose	**hence**	**restore**
....	....	....
....	....	....
....	....	....

Word Form Chart			
Noun	**Verb**	**Adjective**	**Adverb**
series	....	....	....
sequence	sequence	sequential	sequentially

The word *series* is both a singular and plural noun. When it has the meaning of "one set" it takes a singular verb. When the meaning is "two or more sets," it takes a plural verb.

A **series** of lectures is planned for next semester. (singular)

Two **series** of lectures are planned for next year, one in each semester. (plural)

The words *series* and *sequence* are synonyms. *Series* generally refers to "a number of things that come one after another and are of the same type or connected," as in *a series of days* or *a television series*.

A film is a **series** of images displayed at fast speed.

Sequence is usually used for "a number of related actions or events that happen or come one after another," as in *a sequence of odd numbers*. A sequence usually has an order that follows some inner logic or relationship pattern.

Film creates the illusion of movement by putting together a **sequence** of frames in which actions progress very slightly from one to the next.

C. Decide whether these things are or involve a series (*S*) or a sequence (*Q*). Use your dictionary to check the meanings of new words. Discuss your decisions with a partner. Think of one more series and sequence.

.... 1. issues of a monthly magazine   .... 4. a soap opera

.... 2. events leading up to a discovery   .... 5. Spiderman comic books

.... 3. operating a camera   .... 6. driving from one place to another

Series: ....

Sequence: ....

What is the difference between *transit* and *transition*?

Transit is usually used to refer to "the act of moving or being taken from one place to another." Some common terms are *mass transit* and *rapid transit*, which refer to forms of transportation that carry people.

> *Edgerton produced dramatic still photographs of fast-moving objects in* **transit**, *such as bullets in flight.*

Transition is generally used more to talk about the process of "change from one condition or form to another."

> *StroMotion allows viewers to fully appreciate the technique and the quality of aerial maneuvers and highlights the different phases and their* **transitions**.

A person or thing in *transit* is moving or traveling from one place to another.

A person or thing in *transition* is changing form or nature in some way.

D. What types of transitions might these things go through? Discuss your ideas in a small group.

1. a caterpillar
2. a teenager
3. a small business
4. an ambitious worker
5. a senior citizen
6. a story someone thinks of

STEP II VOCABULARY ACTIVITIES: Sentence Level

Hence has two common functions. Sometimes it is a logical transition word, meaning "as a result."

> *These dolls were handmade;* **hence**, *they are expensive.*

It is also a shortened form of the word *henceforth*, meaning "from now on" or "in the future," though this usage is becoming somewhat formal and old-fashioned.

> *Today everyone is excited about fashion trends that will be boring and out of style a year* **hence**.

E. Complete these sentences using the word *hence*.

1. He ate a lot of sweet, fatty foods and never exercised; hence, ...

....

2. The team's star player was injured the day before the big game; hence, ...

....

3. When she was young she was stung by a bee; hence, ...

....

4. Both of his parents were musicians; hence, ...

....

5. A = B and B = C; hence, ...

Before digital photography was invented, photographers had to allow film to be struck by light—they had to *expose* film—in order to capture an image.

*After first **exposing** the film, photographers used a series of chemicals to develop the image.*

More generally, *expose* means to show something or make something visible. Usually this is something hidden, concealed, or previously unknown.

*The bright lights **exposed** all the cracks and lines on the wall.*

Note: *Expose* and *display* are both synonyms of *show*, but *display* is generally used to talk about showing things to make them look good, possibly to sell something or attract attention. *Expose* is often used to show something shameful, corrupt, immoral, or dishonest that had been hidden or disguised.

F. In your notebook, rewrite these sentences using the cues in parentheses. Check your dictionary for help with new words and meanings. Be prepared to read aloud or discuss your sentences in class.

.... 1. The heavy rains have eroded the riverbank. Now all the roots of the trees and bushes are bare. (*expose*)

The heavy rains have washed away the riverbank and exposed the tree roots.

.... 2. Before coming to the city for school, she had never had the opportunity to appreciate the arts. (*exposure*)

.... 3. The politician had to resign after the newspaper found out about his questionable financial deals and published the information. (*exposé*)

.... 4. Parents sometimes allow their children to catch a contagious disease, like measles or chicken pox, so that they will be immune to the disease as adults. (*be exposed to*)

.... 5. The hikers who got lost in the mountains died because they were out in severe weather for too long. (*exposure*)

.... 6. Be sure to put sunscreen on any uncovered areas so that your skin doesn't burn. (*exposed*)

.... 7. At a home design show, you can get great ideas for decorating your apartment. (*exposition* or *expo*)

.... 8. His clients found out he was a fraud and told the police about how he sold them nonexistent property. (*exposed as a fraud*)

G. Read the sentences in activity F again and decide whether each exposure is positive (*P*) or negative (*N*). Discuss your reasoning in a small group.

H. Self-Assessment Review: Go back to page 65 and reassess your knowledge of the target vocabulary. How has your understanding of the words changed? What words do you feel most comfortable with now?

WRITING AND DISCUSSION TOPICS

1. What is your favorite film, television, theatrical, or literary drama? What makes it so dramatic?

2. Has anything dramatic ever happened to you? Do you think it could be the basis for a film?

3. Photography has expanded human perception in various new ways. What new views of the universe, our planet, or the human body have become available to us through photography? How have these views influenced the way we think about things?

4. Is photography a science, an art form, or both? Support your answer with one or more example photographs.

5. If a human being were born with a mutation that caused him to see everything in StroMotion, what kind of advantage might it provide? What kind of disadvantage might result? How could this "StroMotion Man" help or harm society?

THE PHYSICS OF FUN

In this unit, you will

- ⮑ read about the engineering behind the development of amusement park rides.
- ⮑ draw conclusions by inferring information from a text.
- ⮑ increase your understanding of the target academic words for this unit:

adult	credit	input	prior	tradition
automate	distort	obtain	regulate	violate
brief	draft	paragraph	revise	

SELF-ASSESSMENT OF TARGET WORDS

Think carefully about how well you know each target word in this unit. Then, write it in the appropriate column in the chart.

I have never seen the word before.	I have seen the word but am not sure what it means.	I understand the word when I see or hear it in a sentence.	I have tried to use the word, but I am not sure I am using it correctly.	I use the word with confidence in either speaking *or* writing.	I use the word with confidence, both in speaking *and* writing.

BEFORE YOU READ

Read these questions. Discuss your answers in a small group.

1. Are you afraid of heights or do you enjoy being up high? What is one experience you've had with visiting a high place?

2. What is your favorite amusement park ride? Describe why you like it and how it makes you feel.

3. What are some things that engineers need to think about when they build something that will hold people?

READ

This article from a popular science magazine tells the story of the first amusement ride.

A Whale of a Wheel

In 1889, France hosted the first *Exposition Universelle*, or World's Fair, in Paris. In every way, the Exposition was so big, so glamorous, so exotic that no one believed anything could ever surpass it. The city of Chicago, Illinois, decided to try.

The Chicago World's Fair was held in 1893, but planning and building started much sooner. The Fair's organizers wanted to show the world that the United States, and specifically Chicago, was just as capable of grand artistic and technological wonders as France. The centerpiece of the Paris Exposition was an elegant tower of steel tapering up to the sky. It was designed by Gustav Eiffel and gave daring visitors a view of Paris that took their breath away. The organizers of the Chicago World's Fair had to come up with something even more magnificent.

Finding a suitable design to rival the Eiffel Tower proved difficult. Architect Daniel H. Burnham was in charge of the project for the Chicago World's Fair. He received dozens of proposals from engineers and architects around the country to build various kinds of towers. One day, he received a **brief** proposal and rough **draft** of plans for something more unbelievable and outrageous than any **prior** proposal. The author of this proposal was George Washington Gale Ferris Jr.

Ferris proposed building a gigantic wheel that people could ride on as it turned. Burnham rejected Ferris's proposal. He could not believe that such a thing could be safe. It must **violate** the laws of physics. Its own weight would surely **distort** the metal beams, causing it to turn irregularly and eventually collapse. Despite Burnham's fears, Ferris knew his design was sound. He knew that equal pressure applied to every spot on the wheel would balance the forces acting on it. Physics was on his side.

Ferris **revised** the proposal three times and drew up many more drafts of engineering plans. He added countless **paragraphs** of detailed explanation on the engineering required. He got other engineers to inspect his plans and confirm their soundness. Ferris finally **obtained** Burnham's approval in December 1892 and began construction immediately. Soon the wheel towered over the city. By opening day in May 1893, the Ferris wheel was already the star of the Chicago's World's Fair.

Robert Graves was a reporter for the newspaper, *The Alleghenian*. He visited the World's Fair and described the Ferris wheel for readers:

What is the principle, the chief principle, on which the wheel is constructed? It is that of a bicycle wheel.... The lower half of the wheel simply hangs from the mighty axle [center bar], and this lower half supports the upper half by means of the steel framework of its two rims [sides].... The wheel, though apparently rigid in its construction, has just enough elasticity to make this method of support possible, and yet not enough elasticity to produce any appreciable trembling or slipping effect.

The first Ferris wheel

The wheel was supported by two 140-foot (43-meter) steel towers. The 45-foot (14-meter) axle was the largest single piece of forged steel at the time in the world. The wheel itself had a diameter of 250 feet (72 meters), a circumference of 825 feet (251 meters), and a maximum height of 264 feet (80 meters). Between the two rims of the wheel, Ferris hung 36 wooden carriages, like railroad cars, that could hold 60 people each. Every car hung from its own axle. This meant that the cars would swing slightly back and forth as the wheel slowly rotated, but they, and the people inside them, always stayed upright.

The Ferris wheel turned by the power of steam. Two huge boilers, located off the main fairgrounds, generated steam and kept it under high pressure. A system of underground pipes delivered the high-pressure steam to a large wheel on the ground under the Ferris wheel. The energy **input** from the steam caused the ground wheel to rotate, which drove the movement of the whole structure.

The ground wheel and the axle of the Ferris wheel were connected to each other by a massive chain that wrapped around them both. The ground wheel and the axle both had a band of raised pieces around them, called sprockets. The links of the chain fit over the sprockets and held the chain in place. As the steam from the boilers

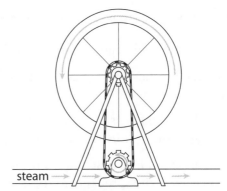

The mechanics of the great wheel

forced the ground wheel to rotate, the chain was pulled along the sprockets. This caused the axle above to rotate as well. The axle then turned the Ferris wheel. A series of brakes and other control devices **regulated** the energy input to keep the wheel's movement smooth and steady.

Ferris was given **credit** for the success of the Chicago World's Fair. His wheel was not only a technological marvel, but a thing of beauty. In fact, the fair's organizers worried that Ferris might have done his job too well. The Ferris wheel seemed too light, too delicate to support itself. History records, however, that the only dangers connected to the Ferris wheel came from the passengers themselves. One passenger, a man named Wherritt, panicked as the wheel began to rotate upwards. He violently crashed around the car until a woman cleverly removed her skirt and threw it over his head. He instantly calmed down. She spoke softly and gently to him until the car returned to the ground and he was helped out.

The influence of Ferris's engineering and entertainment marvel is still clear today. In 1999, London, England, continued the **tradition** of marking momentous occasions by erecting a Ferris wheel. The London Eye, the largest Ferris wheel in the world, was built to celebrate the beginning of the new millennium. On a smaller scale, Ferris wheels of various sizes and types are attractions at fairs and amusement parks around the world. More than a century after it first dazzled visitors at the Chicago World's Fair, the Ferris wheel still has the power to fascinate, thrill, and amaze.

READING COMPREHENSION

Mark each sentence as *T* (true) or *F* (false) according to the information in Reading 1.

.... **1.** The 1889 World's Fair in Paris hosted the first Ferris wheel.

.... **2.** Daniel Burnham first rejected plans for the Ferris wheel because he thought it was unsafe.

.... **3.** People in the Ferris wheel stayed upright as the wheel turned because the carriages they sat in were locked into place and did not move.

.... **4.** A giant chain forced steam from the boilers into the ground wheel, which in turn caused the sprockets to rotate the axle. The axle then turned the Ferris wheel.

.... **5.** Ferris wheels continue to be popular tourist attractions, as evidenced by the construction of the London Eye, the largest Ferris wheel in the world.

READING STRATEGY: Inference

When authors write, they don't always state every idea that they want you to understand. Often, they leave out ideas that they think don't need to be explained. In literature, they do this for artistic reasons. In factual articles, like the ones in this unit, details are usually left out in order to keep the text focused on the most important points.

It is important, however, that you also understand the unstated ideas in a text. Understanding missing information by making guesses is called *inferring*, or making *inferences*. Good readers make inferences based on other ideas in the text and knowledge about the world. This leads to a fuller understanding of the author's ideas and intentions.

Infer the answers to these questions. Then, on the line below, cite evidence from Reading 1 and explain how it supports your inference.

1. Before the Chicago world's fair, what was the general opinion about Chicago?

    a. It was an amazing, exciting city.

    (b.) It was not as impressive as Paris.

    c. It was a smelly, disgusting swamp.

    d. It has a large, beautiful lake.

Evidence: *The Fair's organizers wanted to show the world that the United States, and specifically Chicago, was just as capable of grand artistic and technological wonders as France. (If the organizers felt pressure to prove this, it must mean it was not a generally accepted fact.)*

2. Why did Mr. Wherritt panic?

    a. Looking at the ground far below terrified him.

    b. The swaying motion in the carriage made him sick.

    c. He thought he had gotten into the wrong carriage.

    d. He was not used to being in the same area with women.

Evidence: ....

....

....

3. Why was Ferris's proposal considered outrageous?

    a. It was larger than the other proposals.

    b. It was more expensive than the other proposals.

    c. It seemed physically impossible to build.

    d. It was far more beautiful than the Eiffel Tower.

Evidence: ....

....

....

4. Why did Burnham eventually approve Ferris's proposal?

    a. He knew the wheel would be popular and attract tourists to the fair.

    b. The approval of other engineers helped convince him it would be safe.

    c. He didn't get any other proposals that interested him as much.

    d. He thought it would be more impressive than the Eiffel Tower.

Evidence: ....

....

....

5. Why was the Ferris wheel the star of the fair even before opening day?

    a. Because it was more beautiful than the Eiffel Tower in France

    b. Because it was a lot of fun to ride on a wheel above the city

    c. Because the mechanics of its design were interesting to engineers

    d. Because people could see it being built and got excited about it

Evidence: ....

....

....

STEP I VOCABULARY ACTIVITIES: Word Level

A. Read this passage about an activity that requires precision engineering. Fill in the blanks with the target vocabulary in the box.

credit	prior to	revised
drafted	regulate	violate
input	regulations	
obtain	revise	

Bungee jumping is a popular activity for the thrill-seeking type. It involves jumping from great heights with an elastic rope attached to your ankle. Just (1) .... the moment when you would hit the ground, the elastic rope snaps you back up into the air.

Originally, a form of bungee jumping was practiced by people living on a few islands in the South Pacific. Modern bungee jumpers have (2) .... the materials and methods of the sport and transformed it into a huge commercial enterprise around the world.

Bungee jumping businesses employ people with a strong knowledge of engineering to (3) .... data on many different aspects of the activity: the distance of the drop, the elasticity of the ropes, the effects of factors such as weather conditions and a person's weight and height. These engineers seek the (4) .... of other experts, and even the bungee jumpers themselves, to help them create safe conditions.

Because of the danger involved in the sport and the complicated nature of the calculations involved, some states have (5) .... legislation to (6) .... the bungee jumping industry. These lawmakers deserve (7) .... for improving safety standards. The bungee jumping industry welcomes these (8) .... , since they clarify the steps they need to take to improve safety. Companies that (9) .... the regulations can be sued by injured customers. Most states continue to (10) .... their laws as they learn more about the physics of bungee jumping.

B. What is your opinion? Circle the answer that best reflects what you think. Discuss your answers with a partner.

1. Which of these is the *briefest* activity for people your age?
   a. Eating lunch on a school or work day
   b. Getting ready for the day in the morning
   c. Having a phone conversation with their mother or father
2. Which of these is the worst thing to *violate*?
   a. A company or school policy
   b. An agreement with a friend
   c. The trust of a family member
3. Which of these is the most difficult thing to *draft*?
   a. Plans to build a house
   b. A chapter for a book
   c. A piece of legislation
4. Which of these things is the most difficult to *obtain*?
   a. A high-paying job
   b. An advanced degree
   c. Power over others
5. Which of these actions can most improve a *paragraph*?
   a. Revising it
   b. Rewriting it completely
   c. Leaving it alone

C. Put a check (✓) next to the activities that you think should be regulated by the government. Then, in a small group, choose the five that are most important to regulate, with *1* as the most important and *5* as the least important of the five. Share your answers with the class.

.... selling cigarettes
.... wearing seatbelts in a car
.... owning a gun
.... having children
.... wearing a bicycle helmet

.... owning pets
.... place of residence
.... daily water use
.... eating unhealthy foods
.... violent movies

STEP II VOCABULARY ACTIVITIES: Sentence Level

D. Choose the best collocation (words that go together) in parentheses to complete the sentence. Write the complete sentences in your notebook. Compare sentences with a partner.

1. Information (*obtained by* / *obtained with* / *obtained against* / *obtained for*) child safety researchers indicates that many playground designs are unsafe for children.

2. Playgrounds are (*credited for* / *credited in* / *credited with* / *credited to*) causing over 150,000 accidents each year, most of which are due to design flaws like inappropriately high structures or unnecessarily hard surfaces.

3. These poorly designed playgrounds exist partly because few states have drafted (*regulations on* / *regulations against* / *regulations with* / *regulations from*) playground safety.

4. The U.S. Department of Education tries to ensure that school playgrounds do not violate any of the engineering standards set for child safety, but it does not give (*input in* / *input from* / *input on* / *input for*) public parks.

5. As parents become more concerned about outdoor play equipment that they purchase for their children, some companies have begun to cover their packaging with (*paragraphs at* / *paragraphs from* / *paragraphs of* / *paragraphs to*) explanation about the safety standards they use to design their products, or, at the very least, a brief list of its safety features.

E. Read this story about another kind of entertainment that uses physics for fun. Then, rephrase the sentences in your notebook using the target vocabulary in parentheses. There may be several possible answers. Compare sentences with a partner.

1. A Canopy Tour is an activity in which people travel in short sliding jumps on a system of cables and platforms through the tops of the trees in a rainforest. (*brief*)

   A Canopy Tour is an activity in which people travel in brief sliding jumps on a system of cables and platforms through the tops of the trees in a rainforest.

2. It is not descended from a local ancient cultural ritual, but originated in Central America in the 1970s, when it was developed by scientists to research local plants and wildlife that were previously inaccessible. (*tradition, prior*)

3. As Canopy Tours have developed into tourist attractions in a variety of tropical locales, many businesses have received permission to operate them. (*obtained*)

4. As the tours increase in popularity, different countries have developed a variety of rules for safety—some stricter than others—and the Association for Challenge Course Technology in the United States helps inform consumers about which tour programs break these rules. (*regulations, violate*)

5. In addition, groups of tour providers have written voluntary guidelines with sections detailing regulations for guide training, equipment standards, and safety inspections. (*drafted, paragraphs*)

To *distort* means "to change the shape or sound of something." *Distortion* is the result.

*The old mirror is not flat, so it **distorts** my reflection and makes me look very tall.*

It is often used in a more figurative way, to mean "misrepresent."

*Many people felt the politician **distorted** the facts in order to sway public opinion in his favor.*

F. Reword these sentences using a form of *distort*. Compare your sentences with a partner.

1. When cartographers make maps, they have to change the shape of countries and oceans in order to make a three-dimensional object fit in two dimensions.

   When cartographers make maps, they have to distort countries and oceans in order to represent a three-dimensional planet in two dimensions.

2. With maps that use the Mercator Projection, the north-south and east-west angles have the same amount of stretching, which makes land masses far from the equator appear unusually large.

3. Although use of the Mercator Projection has been criticized as causing the production of inaccurate shapes, it has been used for many years and is still very popular.

4. Recently, developers in Dubai used the Mercator Projection to change the shape of the coastline, creating "The World," a group of man-made islands that look like land masses on a map of the world.

5. Islands representing different countries can be bought by private owners, who can then further change their shapes, creating tourist attractions and amusements.

BEFORE YOU READ

Read these questions. Discuss your answers in a small group.

1. Have you ever been on a roller coaster? If so, what was that experience like? If not, why not? Would you like to ride on one?

2. Do you think most amusement park rides are safe? Why or why not?

3. What effect do roller coasters and other rides have on the body? How are these effects different from the normal stresses people experience every day?

READ

This article from *Popular Mechanics* magazine discusses the physics of safety related to the engineering of thrill rides.

Thrill Rides, or Kill Rides?

Every year, new roller coasters are built that are bigger, faster, and wilder than ever. Tower rides are dropping us farther. Flat rides are spinning us with unimaginable new twists. It all seemed like good clean fun until June 2, 2001. A 28-year-old woman was found unconscious after a three-minute ride on the Goliath roller coaster at Six Flags Magic Mountain in Valencia, California. Paramedics rushed her to a nearby hospital, where she was pronounced dead. The Los Angeles County coroner attributed her death to a pre-existing condition. The woman had a brain aneurysm[1] that could have broken at any time.

Rather than calm people, the coroner's ruling created a controversy that may continue for years to come. The death was one of fifteen fatalities or serious brain injuries that had occurred over the prior ten years among otherwise healthy people who had just taken thrill rides.

By the tens of thousands, children and **adults** line up for thrill rides in amusement parks around the world. These rides are designed to provide the extreme physical sensations you just don't get walking down the street. To find out whether riders need to be as fit as jet pilots to handle the thrills, *Popular Mechanics* asked one of the people best qualified to answer, Captain David L. Steinhiser. He is a flight surgeon for the U.S. Air Force Thunderbirds. "We fly visiting media representatives, who are everyday people, in our jets and subject them to g-forces[2] in excess of those found on roller coasters. We have not had any instances of brain trauma[3]," Steinhiser said. "As fliers, we train to handle and tolerate the heavy g-forces, as high as nine g's. Our visitors will experience sustained g-forces of more than twice the forces found on a roller coaster with no lasting ill effect." But Steinhiser adds that they always screen these people prior to flights to be sure they're healthy.

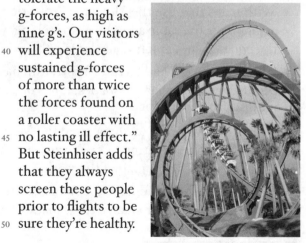

Extreme roller coaster

---

[1] *aneurysm*: a weak spot in an artery in the brain
[2] *g-force*: a unit of measure for acceleration (one "g" is equal to the pull of Earth's gravity)
[3] *trauma*: physical injury

Would Air Force-style preflight medical screening have saved any of those who died soon after coaster rides? That will remain a matter of speculation, but it does raise the question of whether more regulations are needed on thrill rides. The amusement industry doesn't think so, and the scientific evidence that exists appears to concur[4].

The latest evidence to support the amusement industry's position appeared in the October 2002 issue of the *Journal of Neurotrauma*. University of Pennsylvania scientists Dr. Douglas H. Smith and David F. Meaney coauthored the article, "G-Forces, Roller Coasters, and Brain Trauma: On the Wrong Track?" Smith is a brain trauma researcher who studies the effects of automobile crashes. Meaney is a bioengineer who studies brain trauma.

"According to our data," says Smith, "it is unlikely that amusement rides cause brain injuries." The team took g-force data from three high-g-force roller coasters and input the data into a mathematical model for head accelerations. They then compared the results to known thresholds[5] for various types of head injuries. They found that the highest head accelerations from roller coaster rides were far below the minimum thresholds for other types of injuries.

U.S. Consumer Product Safety Commission (CPSC) statistics support Smith and Meaney's results. While injuries and occasional fatalities do occur, they are primarily a result of a ride malfunction or from rider horseplay[6].

Statistically, amusement parks are still one of the safest places to have fun. According to the most recent data provided by the CPSC and the National Sporting Goods Association, in the year 2000 there were far fewer emergency room-treated injuries per 1000 visits at amusement parks than there were for many other recreational activities. In that year, the CPSC estimates,

there were 6,594 emergency room-treated injuries related to amusement park rides. Most of those were minor. In comparison, each year an estimated 20,000 people are treated for injuries sustained at music concerts. And about 200,000 school children visit emergency rooms for injuries sustained on a playground.

The low incidence of injury on rides is credited largely to one organization. Since 1978, the American Society for Testing and Materials (ASTM) has worked with numerous members of the U.S. amusement industry to draft standards and regulations for rider safety. The manufacturers and the ASTM also obtain and analyze data on g-forces. They use this data to revise the design and construction of rides.

One important aspect of their work has to do with the relationship between g-forces and the height and speed of the coasters. The surprising fact is that there is no relationship. G-forces are created by how tightly one changes direction while in motion. When a roller coaster train goes faster, it also goes through a larger radius turn in order to maintain the same g-force as a slower train rolling through a tighter curve. And so, even though advances in technology have led to faster and more thrilling rides, g-force levels on roller coasters have not changed much in the past two to three decades. Today's machines also benefit from the use of computer programs that **automatically** calculate g-forces along every section of the ride.

The issue of g-forces on the body was explored in detail in a classic medical study published nearly a decade ago in the medical journal *Spine*. In their investigation, doctors and engineers found that the normal movements we go through every day subject us to far greater gravitational pull than that felt on any amusement park ride. According to the study, adults experience 10.4 g's when they drop down quickly into a chair. Hopping off a step generates 8.1 g's. A cough is

---

[4] *concur*: confirm, support, agree

[5] *threshold*: limit

[6] *horseplay*: rough or reckless playful behavior

a 3.5-g experience; a sneeze generates 2.9 g's. By comparison, amusement rides average about 4 g's.

Dr. Smith explains that it is not the g-force itself, but how that force is delivered and how briefly it is sustained. "In an auto accident, sudden stopping creates extremely high g-forces, causing brain deformation. If the brain is deformed rapidly, various types of injuries to the brain will occur." This sort of sudden and violent brain distortion is found in car crashes. "We see auto crashes well documented, but that's been extrapolated[7] to roller coasters without any scientific link."

The causal relationship between brain injuries and amusement rides has been widely questioned, however. The Brain Injury Association of America set up a panel of neurologists and other experts to assess the situation. They wanted to determine what is safe and healthy when it comes to g-forces on roller coasters. Their conclusion, issued in winter 2002–03, is that it is safe to ride.

Not everyone is convinced. New Jersey, for example, has decided to establish state regulations in the absence of industry regulations. The limits in New Jersey require that the rider is not subjected to more than 5.6 g's for more than one second per instance. But no amusement park ride in the United States is in violation of this requirement. It is about the same as the voluntary standards created by the ASTM, which the industry supports. In other words, New Jersey's regulation reflects the traditional standard that ride manufacturers have always used. There may be a few rides in development that might match or exceed this limit, but they have yet to appear and probably never will.

[7] *extrapolate*: project data from one thing onto another, generalize

READING COMPREHENSION

Mark each sentence as *T* (true) or *F* (false) according to the information in Reading 2.

.... 1. G-forces on roller coasters are higher than those on Air Force planes.

.... 2. Most injuries on roller coasters occur because of problems with machinery or rider behavior.

.... 3. Scientists are certain that medical screening before roller coaster rides would save lives.

.... 4. The faster a roller coaster travels, the stronger the g-force that riders experience.

.... 5. The length of time over which a g-force is delivered affects the severity of injury to the person experiencing the force.

READING STRATEGY

Answer these questions in your notebook. You will need to make inferences. Support your inferences with evidence from Reading 2. Discuss your answers and inferences with a partner.

1. How do Smith and Meaney's findings support the argument that roller coasters are safe?
2. How do the CPSC findings support the argument that roller coasters are safe?
3. Are the New Jersey regulations for roller coasters necessary? Why or why not?

STEP I VOCABULARY ACTIVITIES: Word Level

A. Read these excerpts from another article about New Jersey's safety regulations on amusement parks. For each excerpt, cross out the one word or phrase in parentheses with a different meaning from the other three choices. Use a dictionary to help you understand new words. Compare your answers with a partner.

1. According to New Jersey's plan, g-forces on a new ride must not exceed limits outlined in the state's g-force table. New rides that exceed those limits are not (*clearly* / *immediately* / *instantly* / *automatically*) rejected, but will be subject to a more extensive review.

2. The plan is based partly on research done in Russia. Legislators there have (*written* / *accepted* / *drafted* / *composed*) a set of (*regulations* / *rules* / *structures* / *policies*) based on military aviation tests on physically healthy (*adult* / *grown* / *mature* / *serious*) individuals.

3. New Jersey regulators also looked at research done in Europe on neck injuries, although this research studied only the (*usual* / *traditional* / *dangerous* / *conventional*) gravity-driven coasters, not the newer, potentially more dangerous coasters.

4. New Jersey regulators relied on research from other countries because they were unable to (*review* / *acquire* / *obtain* / *get*) injury records for the 150 U.S. roller coasters that they studied.

B. Which of these tasks have been automated? Discuss your answers with a partner.

.... washing dishes   .... washing clothes

.... brushing your teeth   .... cleaning the floor

.... walking a dog   .... mending torn clothes

.... answering the phone   .... feeding a child

.... making coffee   .... brushing your hair

C. Most societies regulate certain activities that can be done only by adults. Some also have activities that can only be done by children. Next to each item below, write

  A for activities regulated for adults

  C for activities regulated for children

  B if an activity is regulated for both adults and children

  N if no regulation exists.

Compare answers with a partner. Discuss how each item is regulated, who is responsible for the regulation, and how regulation changes in different contexts.

.... earn money for working   .... get a secondary school degree

.... stay at home alone   .... open a bank account

.... ride the bus alone   .... have an email address

.... drive a car   .... watch a violent movie

.... get married   .... play on a sports team

.... buy cigarettes

D. Complete the passage using the target vocabulary in the box.

brief	input	prior to	violated
credit	paragraph	revise	

Many amusement parks ask for (1) .... from lawyers when creating their safety policies. They want to protect guests from danger, but they also want to prevent injured customers from taking them to court. For example, while waiting in line, park visitors may see a sign posted near the entrance with a lengthy (2) .... explaining who should or should not go on this ride. Guests may also have to watch a (3) .... safety demonstration (4) .... getting on the ride. Then, if riders are injured, the park cannot be held responsible for the injury. The park can show that the visitors knew the safety policies but (5) .... them anyway.

A lawsuit from an injured rider can damage the reputation of an amusement park for years. Legal advisers carefully (6) .... the warnings on a regular basis to make sure they are up to date and cover every possible problem. Park owners (7) .... their strict safety policies and the help of their legal advisors with protecting their good name and their profits.

STEP II VOCABULARY ACTIVITIES: Sentence Level

E. Most countries have regulations that describe how people should behave when they drive cars. In the boxes on the left, write examples of driving regulations that you think are important. On the right, write examples of punishments that you think would be appropriate for people who violate those regulations.

Driving Regulation	Penalty for Violation
No driving while under the influence of alcohol.	*5 years in jail*

F. Imagine that you have the chance to interview the inventor of one of the rides described in this unit. What would you ask? Write interview questions using as many of the target words in this unit as you can. You might have to do some research online. Consider these issues as you prepare your interview questions:

- how the ride works
- what it looks like
- why people like it
- the history of how the inventor developed this ride
- what sort of safety guidelines it requires

Be prepared to use your questions to role play an interview with a partner in class.

G. Think of a traditional game you are familiar with and that you think a visitor from another part of the world would find interesting. Write a brief description of it in the chart. Then, consider what safety regulations would be necessary for people taking part in it for the first time. Be prepared to present your ideas to the class or discuss them in a small group.

Traditional Game	Regulations
Hopscotch—draw boxes on the ground with different numbers and throw a rock into one of the boxes. Then, hop on one leg in all the boxes, except the one with the rock.	1. Do not throw the rock at other people. 2. Wear athletic shoes so you don't twist your ankle. 3. Draw the hopscotch boxes on soft mats so people who fall don't hurt themselves.

H. Self-Assessment Review: Go back to page 81 and reassess your knowledge of the target vocabulary. How has your understanding of the words changed? What words do you feel most comfortable with now?

WRITING AND DISCUSSION TOPICS

1. What is your most pleasant memory of an amusement park? Apart from the rides, what is the best thing about an amusement park? Why do you think so?

2. Have you ever had a bad experience on an amusement park ride? Do you know of someone else who was hurt on a ride? What happened?

3. Compare some experience in your life to an amusement park ride. How did your life experience mirror the ride? What feelings did it create in you? What emotions did you experience?

4. What would a roller coaster look like if a non-engineer designed it, for example, a scuba diver, or a small child, or a dog? Choose any "designer" you want, and use your imagination.

5. What kinds of regulations have you encountered at amusement parks? Did you agree with the regulations or find them unnecessary? Why?

MIND WIDE OPEN

In this unit, you will

- ➲ read about the latest developments in brain research.
- ➲ practice annotating and highlighting texts.
- ➲ increase your understanding of the target academic words for this unit:

attach	induce	integrity	obvious	trigger
chapter	initial	internal	scenario	visual
distinct	insight	minor	sphere	

SELF-ASSESSMENT OF TARGET WORDS

Think carefully about how well you know each target word in this unit. Then, write it in the appropriate column in the chart.

I have never seen the word before.	I have seen the word but am not sure what it means.	I understand the word when I see or hear it in a sentence.	I have tried to use the word, but I am not sure I am using it correctly.	I use the word with confidence in either speaking *or* writing.	I use the word with confidence, both in speaking *and* writing.

MORE WORDS YOU'LL NEED

M.R.I.: magnetic resonance imaging—a medical imaging method using magnets

adrenaline: a bodily chemical generated in response to stress

autistic: referring to autism, which is a neurological disorder

paranormal: not scientifically explainable

BEFORE YOU READ

Read these questions. Discuss your answers in a small group.

1. Do you ever think about the way your mind works? How important is it to understand this in your everyday life? In your academic life?

2. Where do you think emotions come from? Are they physical or psychological?

3. What part of the mind or what mental process would you most hate to lose? Why?

READING STRATEGY: Annotating and Highlighting a Text

Annotating—making notes about what you read—will help you understand and remember the material. It will also make it easier to access the information if you need it in the future.

One form of annotation is **highlighting**. You can highlight by underlining parts of the text or by using a light colored marker to mark the text. To highlight, mark only these things as you read:

- main ideas
- key details
- interesting examples
- frequently mentioned people or places
- important dates or locations
- something strange or surprising
- anything you have a question about or disagree with

In the margins of the book—the blank spaces to the left and right of the text—**take notes** or make comments about why you highlighted the things you did. If necessary, use arrows to connect your notes with the highlighted lines.

As you read the texts in this unit, highlight them and take notes in the margins. Lines have been provided to help you.

Read this *New York Times* book review about *Mind Wide Open*, by Steven Johnson. In this book, Johnson gets to know his own mind a little better by using the tools of modern neuroscience.

Book Review: Mind Wide Open
By JONATHAN WEINER

MIND WIDE OPEN:
Your Brain and the Neuroscience of Everyday Life
By Steven Johnson

Until recently, people couldn't look into themselves directly to explore what Gerard Manley Hopkins called our "inscapes[1]." But now we can. With M.R.I.s, PET scans, and many other high-tech mirrors, we can see right through our own foreheads and begin to
5 watch our mental apparatus[2] in action.

The **scenario** for Stephen Johnson's *Mind Wide Open* is this: Johnson makes himself his own test subject to see what the neuroscientists can show us about our attention spans, talents, moods, thoughts, and drives—our *selves*. He got the idea for this
10 voyage of self-discovery a few years ago while he was hooked up to a biofeedback[3] machine. Lying on a couch with sensors[4] **attached** to his palms, fingertips, and forehead made him feel nervous, and he started cracking jokes with the biofeedback guy. The machine was designed to monitor adrenaline levels, like a lie detector
15 machine. With each joke he made, the monitor displayed a huge spike of adrenaline: "I found myself wondering how many of these little chemical subroutines are running in my brain on any given day? At any given moment? And what would it tell me about myself if I could see them, the way I could see those adrenaline spikes on
20 the printout?"

Johnson writes the monthly Emerging Technology column for *Discover* magazine, and is a contributing editor at *Wired*. He knows how to make complicated science clear and easy to follow, and his style is cheerful, honest, friendly—and filled with those nervous
25 jokes. In his last book, "Emergence," he explored the ways in which the complicated behavior of brains, software, cities, and ants can emerge from the vastly simpler behavior of their smallest working parts—from collections of nerve cells, bits and bytes, citizens and ants—to become the webs and **spheres** of efficient mass circuitry[5].

[1] *"inscape"*: a word created from "interior" and "landscape" to describe one's mental workings
[2] *apparatus*: equipment, machinery
[3] *biofeedback*: a process that makes bodily processes perceptible to the senses
[4] *sensor*: A device that responds to a physical stimulus and transmits a corresponding impulse, such as an electrode that picks up a heartbeat and displays it on a screen
[5] *mass circuitry*: the complete pathway that electronic circuits flow through

30   Here he writes about some of the ways that the behavior of what we like to call our *self* emerges moment by moment from all kinds of separate tools and workshops in the brain, which neuroscientists call *modules*.

     Johnson begins with a gift that most of us take for granted: mind
35   reading. Even before we can talk, almost all of us know how to read subtle hints in the faces, voices, and gestures of the people around our cribs. That is, we can do by instinct what neuroscientists are just learning to do with scanners and monitors.

     To learn about his own mind-reading abilities, Johnson takes
40   a famous test devised by the British psychologist Simon Baron-Cohen. In the test, you are shown a series of 36 different pairs of eyes on a computer screen. Each pair has a **distinctive** expression. For each, you have to choose one adjective from a set of four that Baron-Cohen provides. Multiple choice: is this pair of eyes
45   despondent[6], preoccupied, cautious, or regretful? Johnson finds that he has an instant gut reaction to each pair of eyes. But when he looks harder, he feels less and less sure what he sees.

     Our innate ability to read people's faces is outside conscious thought. As with breathing or swallowing, we can't explain how
50   we do it. Baron-Cohen and others believe that the skill depends partly on the *amygdala*, one of the brain's emotional centers. He has made brain scans of people taking his reading-the-eyes test using functional M.R.I., which reveals which parts of the brain are working hardest from moment to moment. When most people try
55   to decode the emotion in a pair of eyes, their amygdalae light up. When autistic patients do it, their amygdalae are much dimmer.

     In other **chapters**, Johnson explores some of the fear messages that are controlled by his amygdala: traumatic fears that were **triggered** by a near catastrophe when a storm blew in a big window
60   in his apartment. He explores our brain chemistry, describing some of the natural drugs that we give ourselves without knowing it: adrenaline, oxytocin, serotonin, dopamine, cortisol. He learns how to recognize which natural high[7] he is riding, or which bad trip[8] he is enduring. He also learns some useful lessons about the ways
65   our brains' drugs affect our memories. There's also a chapter about his sojourn in a $242 million M.R.I. machine, in which he reads a passage by the Nobel Prize-winning neuroscientist Eric Kandel, and then a passage of his own. The test proves that nothing makes a writer's brain light up like reading his own words.

---

[6] *despondent*: very sad

[7] *high*: a feeling of great pleasure or happiness induced by natural chemicals or medications

[8] *trip*: an altered state of consciousness induced by natural chemicals or medications

70 Johnson's preoccupations, the weather systems of his own inner life, keep cycling back chapter after chapter: his horror when that window blew in and almost killed his wife; his moments of tenderness gazing at their sleeping newborn son. As he explores his inner world and the mental modules that help to shape it, we begin
75 to feel that we are right in there with him—and we have a new sense of what it means to be human.

The best chapter is the last, when Johnson analyzes the current view of the mind. It is **obvious** now that Freud's most basic **insight** was correct—there is more going on in there than we are aware of.
80 This is not new news, but Johnson brings it all alive. He concludes, "Even the sanest among us have so many voices in our heads, all of them competing for attention, that it's a miracle we ever get anything done."

This is an entertaining and instructive ride inward to a place that
85 looks less familiar the better we get to know it. As Johnson says, "It's a jungle in there."

"If a lion could talk we would not understand him," Wittgenstein said. *Mind Wide Open* takes the point closer to home. If every part of our brain could talk, we would not understand ourselves.

READING COMPREHENSION

Mark each sentence as *T* (true) or *F* (false) according to the information in the Reading 1. Look at your highlighting and notes to help you.

.... **1.** Steven Johnson wrote *Mind Wide Open* to see what neuroscientists could show us about the mind.

.... **2.** Johnson used himself as a test subject.

.... **3.** In his previous book, Johnson compared the complicated behavior of brains, software, cities, and ants.

.... **4.** Johnson believes that mind reading—the ability to interpret faces, voices, and gestures—is a rare skill.

.... **5.** The book reviewer criticizes Johnson for making simple science confusing and hard to follow.

.... **6.** Johnson believes that our ability to read people's faces is with us from birth.

.... **7.** An M.R.I. displays which parts of the brain are working hardest during a test.

.... **8.** Johnson doesn't believe that the brain's control of the body's natural drugs is important in dealing with fear or preserving memories.

READING STRATEGY

Write a one-paragraph summary of the review in Reading 1 using your annotations and highlighting for reference. Answer these questions in your summary.

1. Is the review positive or negative?
2. How does the mind-reading test work?

STEP I VOCABULARY ACTIVITIES: Word Level

A. Match the dictionary definitions for the word *attach* with the example sentences. Then, answer the questions that follow. Discuss your answers with a partner.

Definitions	Sample sentences
.... **1.** To fasten or connect one thing to another	**a.** Scientists attached no significance to the threat.
.... **2.** To think something or someone has a particular quality	**b.** She is attached to her family.
.... **3.** To feel a close connection with something or someone	**c.** Several files and some photos have been attached to this email.
.... **4.** To combine electronic files for the purpose of transmission	**d.** He attached the wires from the amplifier to the speakers

1. What have you recently attached to something else (not email)?

....

2. What type of things do you send as email attachments?

....

3. What do you attach a lot of importance to?

....

4. What do you attach little or no importance to?

....

5. Who do you feel attached to?

....

6. What do you feel attached to?

....

B. Put each word in the box in the correct column, based on which target word it is a synonym for. Use your dictionary to check the meanings of new words. Compare your results with a partner.

activate	cause	different	spark
add	clear	distinguishing	special
adhere	connect	fasten	start
apparent	conspicuous	plain	unique

obvious	trigger	attach	distinctive
....	*activate*	....	....
....	....	....	....
....	....	....	....
....	....	....	....

STEP II VOCABULARY ACTIVITIES: Sentence Level

> The word *obvious* means "easily seen or understood." In essay writing, *obvious* and *obviously* can help you avoid longer phrases like "everyone knows" or "it's easy to see," and they can give your ideas an attitude of formality and authority.
>
> **Obviously**, the Internet has aided globalization.
>
> It is **obvious** that the Internet has aided globalization.

C. Complete the statements. Refer to Reading 1 for information. Compare your work with a partner.

1. Obviously, the human mind is ....

   ....

2. It is obvious that modern technology ....

   ....

3. It is obvious that author Steven Johnson is ....

   ....

4. Obviously, the book critic is recommending *Mind Wide Open* because

   ....

   ....

The word *insight* refers to someone's or something's understanding of the true nature of another person or thing. It usually takes the preposition *into*.

> *The math teacher at their middle school has great **insight** into teenagers. She can always figure out how to get them to do their work and perform well.*

Insight can be given (or can attempt to be given) to others. Books, in particular, are often described as having or giving insight.

> *The book gives a good **insight** into the lives of the poor in early 19th-century Europe.*

In other words, the book's author has explained his insight on this subject well. People who read the book are likely to come away with a greater understanding of the topic.

D. Write questions about insight using the cues provided. Answer the questions in complete sentences. Then discuss your answers in a small group.

1. parents / children

    What insights might parents have into their children?

    Parents have insight into their children's likes and dislikes. They know, for example, what foods their kids will probably like, based on other things they like.

2. book about psychology / unhappiness

3. best friends / each other

4. veterinarian / animal behavior

5. babysitter / family problems

6. anthropologist / workplace politics

BEFORE YOU READ

Answer these questions. Discuss your answers in a small group.

1. Have you ever had a strange experience that you could not explain? For example, did you ever sense that someone was watching you? What did you feel at the time? How did you feel later?

2. Did you or someone you know ever have an out-of-body experience (where you felt that you had left your body then returned to it)? What was it like?

3. If you could leave your body then return to it, would you do it? Why or why not? What might you learn from this experience?

READ

This *New York Times* article questions whether unexplained experiences might, in fact, have an explanation.

Out-of-Body Experience?
Your Brain Is to Blame

They are eerie[1] sensations, more common than one might think: A man describes the distinct feeling of a shadowy figure standing behind him, then turns around to find no one there. A woman feels herself leaving her body and floating in space, looking down on her
5 physical body.

People often attribute such experiences to paranormal forces outside the sphere of material life. But according to recent work by neuroscientists, they can be **induced** by delivering mild electric current to specific spots in the brain.

10 In one woman, for example, a zap to a brain region—the angular gyrus—resulted in a sensation that she was hanging from the ceiling, looking down at her body.
15 In another woman, electrical current delivered to the same area triggered a feeling that someonewas behind her,
20 intent on interfering with her actions.

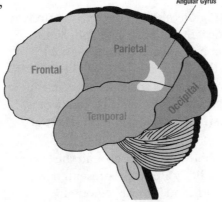

The angular gyrus—a multisensory processing center in the brain

---

[1] *eerie*: strange and frightening

The two women were being evaluated for epilepsy surgery at University Hospital in Geneva, Switzerland. Doctors implanted electrodes into their brains to find the abnormal tissue causing
25 their seizures[2]. As each electrode was activated, stimulating a different patch of brain tissue, the patient was asked to say what she was experiencing.

Dr. Olaf Blanke, a neurologist at the École Polytechnique Fédérale de Lausanne in Switzerland, who carried out the
30 procedures, said that the women had normal psychiatric histories and that they were stunned by the bizarre nature of their experiences.

But this is not a film scenario, and there is nothing mystical about these ghostly experiences, said Peter Brugger, a
35 neuroscientist at University Hospital in Zurich. Dr. Brugger is an expert on phantom[3] limbs—the sensation of still feeling a limb that has been amputated.

"The research shows that the self can be detached from the body and can live a phantom existence on its own, as in an out-of-body
40 experience, or it can be felt outside of personal space, as in a sense of a presence," Dr. Brugger said.

Scientists have gained new understanding of these odd bodily sensations as they have learned more about how the brain works, Dr. Blanke said. For example, researchers have discovered that
45 some areas of the brain combine information from several senses. Vision, hearing, and touch are **initially** processed in the primary sensory regions (eyes, ears, fingertips, etc). But then they flow together, like tributaries into a river, to create the wholeness of a person's perceptions. For example, a dog is **visually** recognized far
50 more quickly if it is simultaneously accompanied by the sound of its bark.

These multisensory processing regions also build up perceptions of the body as it moves through the world, Dr. Blanke said. Sensors in the skin provide information about pressure, pain, heat, cold,
55 and similar sensations. Sensors in the joints, tendons, and bones tell the brain where the body is positioned in space. Sensors in the ears track the sense of balance. And sensors in the **internal** organs, including the heart, liver, and intestines, provide an assessment of a person's emotional state.
60 Real-time information from the body, the space around the body and the subjective feelings from the body are also represented in multisensory regions, Dr. Blanke said. And if these regions are

---

[2] *seizure*: involuntary loss of control sometimes accompanied by violent movements, associated with the disease epilepsy
[3] *phantom*: thought of as real but actually not real

directly stimulated by an electric current, as in the cases of the two women he studied, the **integrity** of the sense of body can be
65 altered.

As an example, Dr. Blanke described the case of a 22-year-old student who had electrodes implanted into the left hemisphere of her brain in 2004.

"We were checking language areas," Dr. Blanke said. The woman
70 suddenly turned her head to the right. That made no sense, he said, because the electrode was nowhere near areas involved in the control of movement. Instead, the current was stimulating the angular gyrus, which blends vision with body sense.

Dr. Blanke applied the current again. Again, the woman turned
75 her head to the right. "Why are you doing this?" he asked.

The woman replied that she had a weird sensation that another person was lying beneath her on the bed. The figure, she said, felt like a "shadow" that did not speak or move; it was young, more like a man than a woman, and it wanted to interfere with her.

80 When Dr. Blanke turned off the current, the woman stopped looking to the right, and said the strange presence had gone away. Each time he reapplied the current, she once again turned her head to try to see the shadow figure.

When the woman sat up, leaned forward and hugged her knees,
85 she said that she felt as if the shadow man was also sitting and that he was clasping her in his arms. She said it felt unpleasant. When she held a card in her right hand, she reported that the shadow figure tried to take it from her. "He doesn't want me to read," she said.

90 Because the presence closely simulated the patient's body posture and position, Dr. Blanke concluded that the patient was experiencing an unusual perception of her own body, as a double. But for reasons that scientists have not been able to explain, he said, she did not recognize that it was her own body she was
95 sensing.

This impression of a mimicking, shadowy self-simulation can occur without electrical stimulation to the brain, Dr. Brugger said. It has been described by people who undergo sensory deprivation, as in mountaineers trekking at high altitude or sailors crossing the
100 ocean alone, and by people who have suffered **minor** strokes or other disruptions in blood flow to the brain.

Six years ago, another of Dr. Blanke's patients underwent brain stimulation to the angular gyrus. The patient experienced a complete out-of-body experience.

105 When the current flowed, she said: "I am at the ceiling. I am looking down at my legs."

When the current ceased, she said: "I'm back on the table now. What happened?"

Because the woman's felt position in space and her actual
110 position in space did not match, her mind searched for the best way to turn her confusion into a coherent experience, Dr. Blanke said. She concluded that she must be floating up and away while looking downward.

Some schizophrenics[4], Dr. Blanke said, experience paranoid
115 delusions[5] and the sense that someone is following them. They also sometimes confuse their own actions with the actions of other people. While the cause of these symptoms is not known, he said, multisensory processing areas may be involved.

When otherwise normal people experience bodily delusions,
120 Dr. Blanke said, they are often completely confused. The felt sensation of the body is so real, so familiar, that people do not realize it is a creation of the brain.

Yet the sense of body integrity is rather easily duped[6], Dr. Blanke said. While it may be tempting to credit the supernatural when this
125 body sense goes wrong, the true explanation is a very natural one. It is the brain's attempt to make sense of conflicting information.

---

[4] *schizophrenic*: a person with *schizophrenia*, a mental disorder in which people confuse reality and imagination
[5] *delusion*: false belief
[6] *dupe*: fool, trick

READING COMPREHENSION

Mark each sentence as *T* (true) or *F* (false) according to the information in Reading 2. Use the dictionary to help you understand new words.

.... 1. Electrical stimulation of the brain can trigger out-of-body experiences.

.... 2. In the tests described, doctors implanted electrodes into the brains of psychologically disturbed and dysfunctional patients.

.... 3. The patients were able to describe their experiences as each electrode was activated.

.... 4. The patients were very surprised by their experiences in this procedure.

.... 5. Neuroscientists believe that out-of-body simulated doubles are actually ghosts with a mystical purpose.

.... 6. The feeling of being with a shadowy presence can only be induced by artificial electrical stimulation.

.... 7. Some areas of the brain combine information from several senses.

.... 8. A person's emotional state is reflected in the condition of internal organs, including the heart, liver, and intestines.

READING STRATEGY

Write a one-paragraph summary of Reading 2 using your annotations and highlighting for reference. Answer these questions in your summary.

1. Are out-of-body experiences generally perceived to be pleasant or unpleasant? Why?

2. How can the integrity, or wholeness, of a person's sense of themselves be altered?

3. How does Dr. Blanke explain out-of-body experiences?

STEP I VOCABULARY ACTIVITIES: Word Level

A. Complete the sentences about neuroscience pioneer Wilder Penfield using the target vocabulary in the box. Use each item one time. The synonyms in parentheses can help you.

attached	induce	minor
chapter	initial	visual
distinctive	insight	

1. Canadian neuroscientist Wilder Penfield conducted the .... *(first)* research into brain mapping in the 1920s and 30s.

2. Penfield discovered that gentle electrical stimulation of the brain could .... the recall of images and sounds from a patient's memory.
   (produce)

3. Although Penfield was interested in mapping both .... and *(seen)* auditory memories, he .... a lot of significance to the large *(assigned)* number and variety of songs in patients' heads.

4. Each time Penfield applied the electrical stimulation, he asked the patient what he/she saw or heard—and thereby learned that each stimulated location held a .... image, sound, or memory.
   (particular)

5. Penfield had the .... to list and map many of the songs people *(intelligence)* had stored in their minds, from radio theme songs and musical show tunes to children's lullabies.

6. Penfield came to believe that the brain retained an almost perfect record of both major and .... experiences from every .... of a *(unimportant)* *(period)* person's life.

The word *sphere* can refer to any round object or something having a round dynamic, like this instance from Reading 1:

*"…brains, software, cities, and ant heaps … become the webs and **spheres** of efficient mass circuitry."*

In Reading 2, *sphere* refers to "an area of interest or activity":

*"People often attribute such experiences to paranormal forces outside the **sphere** of material life."*

The related word *hemisphere* means "half of a sphere." In biology, it is used to refer to the left and right sides of the brain. In politics, it is used to refer to parts of the world.

*Most parts of the brain related to language are in the right **hemisphere**.*

*In the northern **hemisphere**, winter is in December, January, and February.*

B. Categorize these synonyms for *sphere* by definition. (One of the words will be used twice.) Add any other synonyms for *sphere* you can think of to the lists.

| ball | domain | globe | zone |
| circle | field | planet | |

round   **area of interest or activity**

....

....

....

....

C. Complete these sentences using the words in the box. Compare answers with a partner.

| academic sphere | sphere of influence | wider sphere |
| hemispheres | spherical objects | |

1. Artists must be able to draw square, cylindrical, triangular, and
.... , like oranges and balls.

2. Historically, China has had a broad .... in East Asia.

3. The globe can be divided into four .... : Eastern, Western, Northern, and Southern.

4. The professor's work is little known outside the .... of the university.

5. His books are detective stories, but he hopes that they will appeal to a
.... than only mystery lovers.

The adjective *minor* means "not very big, serious, or important, when compared to others." The noun form, *minority*, refers to the smaller number or part of a group.

*A childhood disease resulted in her having a **minor** hearing loss.*

*A small **minority** of the general population has epilepsy.*

The noun *minor* has two meanings. Academically, it means "a field of study chosen as a secondary area of academic specialization." (see Unit 2, *major*)

*She is a biology major with a **minor** in economics.*

These concepts can also be expressed in verb form:

*She is majoring in biology and **minoring** in economics.*

In law, a *minor* is any person who has not yet reached the legal age of an adult.

*It is illegal to sell cigarettes to **minors**.*

D. Give three examples of these things. Discuss your answers with a partner. What makes your examples minor?

1. a minor problem: ....

....

2. a minor injury: ....

....

3. a minor illness: ....

....

4. a minor inconvenience: ....

....

5. a minority group: ....

....

STEP II VOCABULARY ACTIVITIES: Sentence Level

Induce has the meaning "make or persuade someone to do something."

*Nothing could **induce** him to change his mind.*

It can also mean "cause or produce."

*The doctor gave her a drug that **induces** sleep.*

E. What external or internal forces might induce these things? Discuss your answers in a small group. Choose the best three answers and share them with your classmates.

1. laughter

2. sympathy

3. the telling of a secret

4. emigration from your country

5. hardship on a family

6. the loss of a person's mental integrity

> A *scenario* is "one way that things may happen in the future."
>
> People often try to predict possibilities by imagining the *worst-case scenario* and the *best-case scenario*.
>
> *The doctor said that the worst-case **scenario** is that the drugs don't work and her illness progresses quickly.*

F. Read these situations and discuss them with a partner. What is the worst-case scenario and best-case scenario for each? Discuss your ideas in a small group.

1. Your great-aunt is old, very wealthy, and crazy about cats. She has no children and you are her favorite relative.

2. This evening, you are going to meet the parents of your boyfriend or girlfriend for the first time at a fancy, expensive restaurant.

3. You awake to realize that your alarm did not go off. You have slept through a very important test in your most difficult class.

4. Walking along the street toward your home, you get the distinct feeling that someone is following you.

G. Go online and find information about some aspect of the brain not mentioned in this unit. Write a one-paragraph summary of your findings. Be prepared to read aloud or discuss your work in class.

H. Self-Assessment Review: Go back to page 97 and reassess your knowledge of the target vocabulary. How has your understanding of the words changed? What words do you feel most comfortable with now?

WRITING AND DISCUSSION TOPICS

1. Imagine yourself in the mind of some type of animal here on Earth. How might this mind feel and work? What insights might you have that you do not have as a human? Imagine an entire day in this other mind.

2. Compare and contrast the way these work: a mind and a computer.

3. Compare and contrast the way these look and work: a mind and a city.

4. How might the human mind change in the future? What could induce these changes?

5. Choose a movie, book, or video game that deals with paranormal phenomena. Summarize it and include your opinion about the issues it raises.

CHILD PRODIGIES

In this unit, you will

- ➲ read about child prodigies and the challenges they pose for their families and society.
- ➲ learn how to recognize and analyze comparison and contrast in a text.
- ➲ increase your understanding of the target academic words for this unit:

challenge	enormous	factor	normal	reveal
concentrate	environment	focus	pursue	technology
considerable	expert	intelligence	resource	utilize

SELF-ASSESSMENT OF TARGET WORDS

Think carefully about how well you know each target word in this unit. Then, write it in the appropriate column in the chart.

I have never seen the word before.	I have seen the word but am not sure what it means.	I understand the word when I see or hear it in a sentence.	I have tried to use the word, but I am not sure I am using it correctly.	I use the word with confidence in either speaking *or* writing.	I use the word with confidence, both in speaking *and* writing.

MORE WORDS YOU'LL NEED

prodigy: a person who is significantly advanced in a particular area; usually applied to children

society: the people of a particular culture who share general values and priorities

Read these questions. Discuss your answers in a small group.

1. Have you ever known anyone who was very, very smart? What could they do or what did they know that made them different from other people their age?

2. What can a family do to help or encourage a baby's mental development? Physical development? Emotional development?

3. Schools often want to know how intelligent children are. How do schools usually measure intelligence? What kinds of tools or tests do they use? What skills or abilities do they measure?

READ

This magazine article spotlights the unusual abilities of some very special children.

Child Prodigies

It seemed **normal** when Nguyen Ngoc Truong Son wanted to play chess with his parents. However, it was unusual when he **revealed** that he already knew how to play—before anyone
5　taught him. Apparently the two-year-old had learned all of the rules by watching his parents. After only one month of playing with them, he was winning all of the games. By age 4, he was competing in national tournaments. By age 12,
10　he was Vietnam's youngest champion.

Another two-year-old child, Jay Greenberg, likewise surprised his parents by drawing pictures of musical instruments that he had never seen. They soon discovered that Jay
15　"heard music in his head." He began to compose music at age 3. By age 10, he was attending the prestigious Julliard Conservatory in New York, composing full symphonies. Jay was noted not only for the quality of his musical work, but also
20　the speed at which he was able to produce it. That is, while talented professional composers normally write five or six symphonies in a lifetime, Jay wrote five by the age of 12.

A third young child, Abigail Sin, was first
25　introduced to piano lessons at age 5 and had what her tutor called an "unstoppable urge to master the keyboard." She became Singapore's most celebrated pianist by age 10.

Child prodigies such as these are a mystery
30　to **experts** and non-experts alike. On the one hand, they attract praise and attention from everyone they meet; on the other hand, they attract criticism and they find it difficult to fit in with the rest of the world.

35　Child prodigies are highly intelligent, but this is not the only **factor** that sets them apart. They are considered prodigies because of their exceptional ability in one domain, or area. Experts define *prodigy* as "a young child
40　who displays mastery of a field that is usually undertaken by adults." Child prodigies usually appear in structured areas such as language, math, drawing, chess, and music. They are not as likely to appear in less structured domains
45　such as medicine, law, or creative writing, areas that require experience.

Child prodigies can **focus** their attention for long periods of time, **concentrating** on tasks that would bore other children of the
50 same age. Abigail Sin practiced piano at least 25 hours a week. Similarly, two-year-old Nguyen Ngoc Truong Son had the concentration to play chess for hours at a time. The distinction of "prodigy" thus goes beyond mere **intelligence**.
55 For explanations, experts look in two directions: *nature*, the child's unique biology, and *nurture*, the child's **environment**.

When researchers look to *nature* to explain child prodigies, they study innate or inborn
60 qualities. For example, they look at whether the brain structure of a prodigy is different from that of a child with average intelligence. **Technology** is a great help in answering this question. For instance, scientists utilize
65 imaging technology to see the amount of activity in different parts of the brain. These brain scans reveal that the frontal lobe of a prodigy's brain is very active, unlike children with average intelligence doing the same
70 tasks. Their frontal lobes are virtually inactive. Science has proven that the frontal lobe of the brain controls many aspects of thought and concentration. This may explain how prodigies can focus on a task, solve complex
75 problems, and learn quickly.

When researchers look to *nurture* to explain child prodigies, they focus on the child's environment instead of the child's biology. The most important factor on the *nurture* side is the
80 parents. Raising a child prodigy is extremely challenging. It requires **considerable** patience, creativity, and **resourcefulness**.

Some parents are delighted by the extraordinary abilities of their children. They
85 make use of all the resources they have or can find to support them. For example, Jay Greenberg's parents bought their 2-year-old son a cello when he requested it and arranged for music lessons.

90 Other parents are not so supportive of their child prodigy. On the contrary, some parents even see their offspring's gifts as a way to draw attention to themselves and their own interests. Boris Sidis, for example, was a well-
95 known scientist with strong opinions about making the most of one's intelligence and about raising children. When his son Billy was born, Boris saw the child as an opportunity to test his theories.

100 From Billy's birth, it was clear that he was an exceptional child. His parents **utilized** every opportunity to teach him language, math, science, and logic. Boris was very poor, but he used his limited resources to buy or
105 acquire toys and books for the young genius. Billy Sidis spoke five languages at age 5. He passed entry exams for MIT and Harvard Medical School at age 9 and was admitted to Harvard at age 11. He was considered a genius
110 in mathematics, physics, and languages.

Boris claimed that his methods of child-rearing were responsible for his son's abilities and sought publicity. The press, in turn, focused more on the young Harvard student's odd
115 personal life than on his accomplishments. It was soon clear that Billy was unprepared to relate to other people, function successfully in the real world, or manage the **challenges** of being different. After college, he lived an
120 isolated life. Despite his intelligence, he died unemployed and in poverty.

When people are unusual, they attract attention. In the case of child prodigies, the attention they receive is both positive and
125 negative. It is positive because most people admire intelligence. It is negative because prodigies are very different from other people. They are a challenge for teachers, who expect 7-year-olds to prefer Batman to Beethoven.
130 They are a challenge to parents, who want to help them but often lack the resources or find their needs and desires difficult to understand and meet. They present a challenge to scientists, who want to study them without
135 further isolating them from normal society. And they challenge the world because they reveal the tendency that people have to reject those who are different from the norm.

READING COMPREHENSION

Mark each sentence as *T* (true) or *F* (false) according to the information in Reading 1. Use the dictionary to help you understand new words.

.... **1.** The parents of two-year-old Nguyen Ngoc Truong Son taught him to play chess and he learned very quickly.

.... **2.** The parents of Jay Greenberg did not provide an environment that was focused on music, but young Jay had great interest in music at a very young age.

.... **3.** Jay Greenberg wrote symphonies very quickly because he utilized the help of talented professional composers.

.... **4.** The factors that seem to always be present in a child prodigy are 1) an unusually high intelligence and 2) the ability to master one area, such as music or math.

.... **5.** The child prodigies mentioned in the reading showed considerable interest and ability in creative writing.

.... **6.** Technology has revealed that the brains of highly intelligent children are different than the brains of children with normal intelligence.

.... **7.** Child prodigies sometimes select areas of interest that they did not learn from their parents or their environment. This supports the explanation of *nurture*.

.... **8.** All of the parents mentioned in the article provided their children with both educational and psychological resources.

.... **9.** According to the article, people with normal intelligence present fewer challenges to society and are more accepted.

READING STRATEGY: Recognizing Comparison and Contrast

> Writers often compare things and ideas to show how they are similar. They also contrast things and ideas to show how they are different. Comparisons and contrasts are important in helping the reader understand how things and ideas relate to each other. You can recognize comparisons and contrasts by the context clues that signal them.

A. Read these context clues. Write *S* for those that indicate similarity (comparison) or *D* for those that indicate difference (contrast). Compare your answers with a partner.

_S_ both	.... in the same way	.... on the contrary
.... but	.... instead of	.... on the other hand
.... despite	.... likewise	.... similarly
.... however	.... moreover	.... unlike

> Some words signal a contrast between the central meanings of two sentences. Careful reading will often reveal that *words* are also being contrasted.
>
> *Child prodigies attract <u>praise and attention</u> from everyone they meet;* **on the other hand,** *they attract <u>criticism</u> and they find it difficult to fit in with the rest of the world.*

B. Look at these lines from Reading 1. Write the context clue and circle whether it indicates comparison or contrast. Then, write which words are being compared or contrasted.

1. Line 3

   Context clue: *however* .... Comparison or (contrast)?

   Words: *normal / unusual* ....

2. Line 12

   Context clue: .... Comparison or contrast?

   Words: ....

3. Line 32

   Context clue: .... Comparison or contrast?

   Words: ....

4. Line 51

   Context clue: .... Comparison or contrast?

   Words: ....

5. Line 68

   Context clue: .... Comparison or contrast?

   Words: ....

6. Line 78

   Context clue: .... Comparison or contrast?

   Words: ....

7. Line 91

   Context clue: .... Comparison or contrast?

   Words: ....

STEP I VOCABULARY ACTIVITIES: Word Level

A. Read these excerpts from another article on child prodigies. For each excerpt, cross out the one word or phrase in parentheses with a different meaning from the other three choices. Compare your answers with a partner.

1. Parents can create a positive or a negative environment for their highly intelligent children. The mother of 6-year-old Hungarian cellist Janos Starker wanted her son to (*display / concentrate on / focus on / think about*) his music practice, so she made tiny sandwiches and left them on his music stand. She didn't want him to have to get up and look for a snack.

2. Given the results, we should not be critical of this mother's methods. Janos Starker's (*considerable / great / expert / extensive*) success as an international cellist lasted over 50 years and his is one of the great musical careers of our time.

3. Another musician to (*reveal / display / utilize / demonstrate*) exceptional musical promise was pianist Ruth Slezynska. She performed at a major concert for the first time in 1929 at the age of four.

4. Whereas Starker's mother encouraged him with tiny sandwiches, Slezynska's father created (*a feeling / an environment / an atmosphere / a setting*) of fear. He forced her to practice nine hours every day and hit her when she played a wrong note.

5. The abnormal (*isolation / anxiety / pressure / stress*) was too much for the young girl. At 15 she suffered a major breakdown that ended her career.

> The word *resource(s)* refers to something that a person or a country can use. It can be tangible (money, equipment) or intangible (moral support, knowledge).

B. Which of these items would be useful resources for a doctor? Put a check (✓) next to these items. How might a doctor utilize each resource? Discuss your answers with a partner.

.... **1.** books

.... **2.** a computer

.... **3.** another doctor in the family

.... **4.** coal

.... **5.** a microscope

.... **6.** a hammer

.... **7.** knowledge of astronomy

.... **8.** a telephone

C. What are some resources that these people might utilize? Think of as many resources as possible. Discuss your answers in a small group.

1. marathon runner

2. journalist

3. business student

4. kindergarten teacher

> To *reveal* something means "to make something known that was previously secret or unknown." A *revelation* is something important and usually surprising that is revealed.

D. With a partner, discuss these questions: What might each of these people *not* want to reveal? Why? What might result from the revelation?

1. a spy
2. a research scientist
3. a used-car salesman
4. someone you've just met at a party and are attracted to
5. a psychiatrist

STEP II VOCABULARY ACTIVITIES: Sentence Level

Word Form Chart			
Noun	Verb	Adjective	Adverb
challenge	challenge	challenging challenged*	....

E. Answer the questions using each form of *challenge* at least once. Refer to Reading 1 for information. Discuss your answers in a small group or as a class.

1. How did the Greenbergs feel about raising Jay?

   For the Greenbergs, raising a child prodigy was a challenge, but they enjoyed supporting him and encouraging his interests.

2. What were some of the difficulties faced by Billy Sidis in his adult life?

   ....

   ....

3. What difficulties do researchers or experts face as they try to better understand child prodigies?

   ....

   ....

4. What difficulties do child prodigies pose for society?

   ....

   ....

5. In your opinion, why do child prodigies "challenge the world" and the society they live in?

   ....

   ....

---

* When used as an adjective, *challenged* has a different meaning from the other words in its family. It means "having a particular type of difficulty" (for example, *visually challenged* or *physically challenged*). A synonym is *handicapped*. This form is not used in this unit.

Word Form Chart

Noun	Verb	Adjective	Adverb
expertise expert	....	expert	expertly
....	....	considerable	considerably
technology technologist	....	technological	technologically
resource(s)	....	resourceful	resourcefully

F. Read the story about another child prodigy, Chandra Sekar. Then, in your notebook, restate each of the sentences using the words in parentheses. Do not change the meanings of the sentences. Be prepared to present your work to the class.

1. Chandra Sekar grew up in India. Even though his family was too poor to own a computer, he was very interested in technology when he was a toddler. (*considerable*, *technological*)

    Chandra Sekar didn't have a computer, but he showed considerable interest in technological things from a very early age.

2. His father wanted to encourage Chandra's technological skills. (*technology*)

3. He hoped that Chandra would one day become a recognized expert in computers. (*expertise*)

4. His father was poor, but he found ways to earn enough money to buy the young boy a computer when he was only four years old. (*resourceful* or *resources*)

5. Chandra found a way to teach himself to use MS-DOS, LOTUS, and MS-Word. (*technological resources* or *resourceful*)

6. He was only 10 when he became the world's youngest Microsoft Certified Systems Engineer. The average age for engineers is 30. (*considerably*)

7. When he was 11 and a student at a university in Madras, the government of India honored Chandra because he was very knowledgeable about the technology related to computer network security. (*expertise* or *expert*)

G. Imagine you are a journalist and you have a chance to interview Chandra Sekar. Prepare interview questions using the cues provided. Be prepared to act out your interview with a partner.

1. How / environment

    How did your home environment help you succeed?

2. which / factors
3. what / challenges
4. when / intelligent or intelligence
5. how / normal / different
6. why / concentrate or focus / technology
7. where / expertise
8. what / resources
9. who / influence

BEFORE YOU READ

Read these questions. Discuss your answers in a small group.

1. What do you think would be the biggest challenges for parents of a prodigy? Why do you think this is true?

2. Doctors and other experts claim that it is impossible for a child prodigy to live a "normal" life. What do you think they mean by this? Do you agree?

3. Children with high intelligence often score *lower* on standardized tests than do children of normal intelligence. Why do you think this happens?

READ

This *New York Times* article gives advice to parents of child prodigies on how to meet the needs of their extraordinary children.

Not Like Other Kids

Last summer, after serious thought, Toby Rosenberg announced to his friends and family that he was changing his name. "Toby," he felt, was "a little boy's name." Instead, he would
5 be called Karl, like his father before him. His school accepted the switch. His parents had no argument. Toby—now Karl—was 5 years old.

And he had a point: regardless of his age, Karl has never been a little boy. At 14 months, he began
10 to read aloud from the posters he viewed from his stroller. It would be another full year before he talked on his own; but once he did, he spoke fluent English and Polish (his mother, Anna, is from Krakow) and several other languages. He
15 trained himself to write Japanese after studying the label on a bottle. He taught himself the Hebrew alphabet after seeing the characters on a dreidel, a type of toy. Last year, after seeing a book in a museum shop on ancient Egypt, he compiled
20 a dictionary of hieroglyphics. The impression you get when you first meet Karl is that of a bookish teenager, a middle-aged diplomat, and a talkative grandmother trapped together in the body of a first grader.

25 "You don't know what it's like with Karl," his father says, laughing tiredly. Karl Sr. was once an artist, and is now a website designer. He spends at least an hour every afternoon in the family's one-bedroom Brooklyn apartment drafting sketches
30 and submitting them to his son's critiques. "He stands behind me and tells me to draw things over and over to his specifications," Karl says. "If he's not on the Internet, he's here, issuing commands over my shoulder. We just want to encourage
35 his interests and support him any way we can. Nobody in this household is trying to tell him what to do." Which is just as it should be.

Experts offer parents of child prodigies this advice about raising their gifted children:

40 **1. Don't overstructure your child's life.** Experts advise parents of hyper-intelligent children that, instead of filling their time with planned activities, they should try not to be too controlling. "Profoundly gifted kids are highly
45 curious and likely to **pursue** all kinds of interests with great passion," says Sandra Berger, a gifted-education specialist for more than 20 years. "It's best to let the child's interests be your guide."

2. Provide as many learning opportunities
50 **as possible.** Parents should strive to introduce their children to a wide variety of subjects. They should take them on field trips and museum tours; moreover, the child's normal environment should be treated as an experiential playground.
55 It was reportedly his early walks in the woods

with his father that alerted Richard Feynman, the Nobel-prize-winning physicist, to the complexity of life. For Karl, it was drives past the Williamsburg Bridge that piqued his avid interest in construction.

Such interests can prove a distraction. When he was taking his Educational Records Bureau exam in January, Karl spent much of the allotted time lecturing the test-givers on the unusual architecture of the Chrysler Building, which was visible through the classroom window. When the examiners tried to summarize Karl's irregular score, they mentioned his "most noteworthy . . . fund of knowledge."

Of course, even without a standardized-test score, Karl's parents know he's a genius. On the other hand, they know that they should never, ever use that term.

3. Avoid calling your child a genius. "There are three reasons the label could only be unhelpful," says Dr. Jack Shonkoff, an expert on early childhood development. "One, it puts an **enormous** burden on the kid that he or she will have trouble living up to. Two, it's a setup for other people—relatives, teachers—to be disappointed in the kid's future performance. And three, it serves to set the child apart from other children." Shonkoff says that extremely talented kids are pigeonholed, or stereotyped, enough already. They don't need a label to isolate them even more.

4. Don't expect your child to be popular. Combating social isolation may be the greatest challenge for those raising exceptionally intelligent kids. Karl has had a typically uphill battle finding a school—let alone a circle of friends—that can contain him. At 3 years old, he was asked to leave his preschool program at the local Y.M.C.A. His teachers thought that his obvious boredom was a bad influence on the other children. After a search, his parents discovered the East Manhattan

School for Bright and Gifted Children, but the independent school soon closed. Karl then transferred to a first-grade class at a public school in Brooklyn. He was immediately promoted to its accelerated program, but his social life lagged far behind.

It's no surprise. Adults tend to make friendships on the basis of shared interests and coincidental pursuits. Similarly, highly gifted children seek out friends like themselves, rather than falling into groups according to age or grade. "These kids just aren't likely to be part of a huge gang in the lunchroom," Berger says.

5. Don't sacrifice educational advancement to give your child a "normal" upbringing. Holding children back from upper-level grades and early college won't help them socially. On the contrary, it will frustrate them—and their teachers. "These kids will exhaust the resources of any normal classroom," Berger says. "Six-, seven-, and eight-year-olds who are interested in aerospace technology shouldn't be stuck in homeroom[1]."

Karl's extensive, far-flung pursuits could exhaust just about anyone. He's played the piano since he was 3. Two years later he requested a violin, and his parents managed to borrow one. In addition, the family's apartment was cluttered with Karl's drawings of the Titanic, which he reimagined as a medieval galleon, with his floor sculpture of Moscow's St. Basil's Cathedral reconfigured as an ancient Irish church and with the whirling presence of Karl himself.

Preparing to present his well-illustrated, self-assigned report on the Statue of Liberty, he announced to his family: "The architect was Frederic-Auguste Bartholdi; Auguste—I mean—did you hear that? A-goose. I said goose!" He bursts into giggles, and for the moment, at least, Karl Jr. is completely happy and 6 years old.

---

[1] *homeroom*: the room where children gather at the start of the school day and to wait for activities

READING COMPREHENSION

Mark each sentence as *T* (true) or *F* (false) according to the information in Reading 2. Use the dictionary to help you understand new words.

.... **1.** Toby Rosenberg pursued changing his name because he and his parents had a challenging relationship. They did not get along well.

.... **2.** Karl Jr. learned languages before he went to school because his parents utilized the help of private tutors at home.

.... **3.** Karl Jr.'s teachers believed that he was a bad influence on other children because he acted bored.

.... **4.** Child prodigies usually have an enormous number of friends.

.... **5.** Two factors that make life more challenging for bright children are isolation from friends their age and difficulty in finding an appropriate school.

.... **6.** Intelligence comes naturally for child prodigies, but concentration does not.

.... **7.** The article suggests that it is not necessary for parents to select new areas of interest for their children. Highly intelligent children do best when they are allowed to pursue their natural interests.

.... **8.** Most classrooms don't have enough resources to meet the educational needs of exceptionally bright children.

READING STRATEGY

Skim Reading 2 for context clues and record them. Circle whether they indicate comparison or contrast, and write which words or ideas are being compared or contrasted. Compare your findings with a partner.

1. Line(s): ....

Context clue: .... Comparison or contrast?

Words being compared/contrasted: ....

2. Line(s): ....

Context clue: .... Comparison or contrast?

Words being compared/contrasted: ....

3. Line(s): ....

Context clue: .... Comparison or contrast?

Words being compared/contrasted: ....

4. Line(s): ....

Context clue: .... Comparison or contrast?

Words being compared/contrasted: ....

5. Line(s): ....

Context clue: .... Comparison or contrast?

Words being compared/contrasted: ....

STEP I VOCABULARY ACTIVITIES: Word Level

A. Complete the sentences about Albert Einstein using the target vocabulary in the box. Use each item one time. The synonyms in parentheses can help you.

concentrated	expertise	pursued
considerably	factor	revealed
enormous	intelligence	
an environment	normal	

.... **a.** The .... of Albert Einstein is now well
        (very large)   *(mental ability)*
   known, but it wasn't so obvious when he was young.

.... **b.** In school, the young Einstein loved mathematics and science, but he

   .... less on other subjects. He received poor grades in
        (focused)
   history, geography, and languages.

.... **c.** When he was 16, he wrote a paper that .... his early ideas
                                                    (made known)
   about the theory of relativity.

.... **d.** Though it is .... for children to speak before the age of 3,
                           (usual)
   Einstein didn't say his first words until he was nearly 4. He didn't read until

   he was 7, which was .... older than other prodigies such as
                        (much)
   Abigail Sin or Billy Sidis.

.... **e.** As a boy, Einstein's two uncles gave him .... that challenged
                                                       (the surroundings)
   him and encouraged his interest in mathematics and science.

.... **f.** His .... related to his theory continued throughout his life.
              (knowledge)
   He was awarded the Nobel Peace Prize in 1921.

.... **g.** One .... that led to his interest in physics sprang from
              (thing)
   an incident that occurred when he was only five. His uncles showed him a

   compass. From then on, Einstein .... physics with great
                                    (tried to understand)
   passion.

B. Tell the story of Einstein's life by putting the sentences in activity A into a logical order. Number them from *1* to *7* (more than one sequence may be possible). Then, use the target words as you compare stories with a partner.

C. Many academic words are also considered formal words. Which of the target words in this unit (see the list on page 113) are more formal synonyms for these informal words? Be sure to use the right form of the target words.

Informal	Formal
1. smart	....
2. to use	....
3. huge	....
4. uncover	....
5. difficulty	....
6. (specialized) knowledge	....
7. activities or pastimes	....

A word analogy shows the relationship between two pairs of words. First, you identify the relationship between the first pair of words. The relationship is usually synonyms, antonyms, examples, or verb/object:

concentrate : focus	synonyms
heredity : environment	antonyms
psychologist : expert	example
focus : attention	verb/object

To complete an analogy, find a word for the second pair that shows the same relationship as in the first pair of words:

concentrate : focus AS utilize : ....*use*..........

The analogy is read like this: "*Concentrate* is to *focus* as *utilize* is to *use*." This means that the word "concentrate" has the same relationship to the word "focus" as the word "utilize" has to the word "use." *Concentrate* and *utilize* are each a synonym for the other word.

D. Use target vocabulary from this unit (in the correct form) to complete these analogies. Then write the type of relationship each analogy has. Compare your work with a partner's.

Type of relationship

1. intelligent : unintelligent AS normal : ......*abnormal*.......... ...*antonyms*...............

2. a painting : art AS a computer : ....

3. get : receive AS seek : ....

4. car : transportation AS money : ....

5. hide : reveal AS waste : ....

6. show : respect AS focus : ....

E. Read these sample sentences that feature the words *normal* and *norm* and answer the questions below in your notebook, using the dictionary as suggested. Compare your answers with a partner.

- Technology has revealed that the brains of highly intelligent children are different from the brains of children with normal intelligence.
- Child prodigies challenge the world because they reveal the tendency to reject people who seem too different from the norm.
- Experts claim that it is impossible for a child prodigy to live a "normal" life.
- A child prodigy's normal environment should be treated as an experiential playground.
- Don't sacrifice educational advancement to give your child a "normal" upbringing.

1. What are some things that are referred to as *normal* in the sample sentences?

2. Look up the word *normal* in your dictionary and read the sample sentences. What are some other things that are referred to as normal?

3. What is implied when *normal* appears in quotation marks?

4. What is meant by *the norm*? Write a brief definition. Confirm it with your dictionary.

STEP II VOCABULARY ACTIVITIES: Sentence Level

F. In a small group, discuss these questions. Use the dictionary to clarify word meanings, if needed.

1. Think about a culture that you know well. What are the norms for each of these customs? What factors might have caused these norms to develop?

   a. the food eaten for the evening meal

   b. the gifts that are given for a major holiday

   c. the age that young people move away from their families

   d. the amount of money spent on children's education

2. What do you think are the three most important factors to consider when parents are choosing a school for their child?

   .... **a.** location

   .... **b.** number of children in a class

   .... **c.** friendly classroom environment

   .... **d.** the intelligence of the teachers

   .... **e.** the intelligence of the other students

   .... **f.** the school's technological resources

   .... **g.** the condition of the school building

   .... **h.** other: ....

G. Which of these pursuits do you consider most challenging? Rank them from *1* (most challenging) to *4* (least challenging).

.... reading a book in Spanish .... fixing a broken computer

.... cooking dinner for 10 people .... running a 3-mile race

As a class or in small groups, make a chart and tally everyone's answers. Which item does the group find most challenging? Least challenging? Why do you think this is true? What environmental factors do you think might have contributed to the results?

Both hereditary and environmental factors have considerable influence on the person a child becomes. Hereditary factors include the biological traits that people inherit from their parents, such as eye color or height. Environmental factors refer to the things that happen to people after they are born: for example, the way their parents treat them, what they learn and experience, what they eat, where they live, and even illnesses or accidents that occur.

H. Read these factors that have shaped the lives of some child prodigies. Write *H* in the blank for those you think are hereditary factors. Write *E* for those you think are environmental factors. Then explain your answer and how each factor may have affected the child. Present your opinions in a small group.

.... **1.** The parents of Nguyen Ngoc Truong Son make less than $100 a month.

....

....

.... **2.** Jay Greenberg has "heard music in his head" since he was two years old.

....

....

.... **3.** Abigail Sin has a twin brother who is not a child prodigy.

....

....

.... **4.** Billy Sidis spoke five languages at the age of 5, including his father's native Russian.

....

....

The verb *pursue* means to follow something in order to catch it or to work at something in order to accomplish it.

*The police **pursued** the robber in a car chase.*

The noun form, *pursuit*, is often followed by the preposition *of* and a noun.

*My parents are happy about my **pursuit** <u>of a career in business</u>.*

I. Look at these arguments for and against government, or public, involvement in the education of child prodigies. Restate each idea in your notebook, using the word in parentheses. Then, write a paragraph that expresses your own opinion. Try to use as many target words as possible in your work. Be prepared to present your work in class.

For	Against
All children should have the right to realize their highest potential. Therefore, public money should be spent to help prodigies achieve their goals. (*pursuit*)	Public resources are limited. We cannot afford to spend extra money to help child prodigies. (*pursuing*)
Prodigies are a valuable future resource for a society; therefore, the government should help them try to reach their intellectual goals. (*pursue*)	Very few people have prodigies in their families. It is therefore unfair to spend public funds and give special attention to them. (*resources*)
Prodigies are likely to achieve more if more resources are made available to them. Society should do everything in its power to help develop a prodigy's intellect and expertise. (*utilization*)	In the interest of equal education for all children, extra resources should not be given to child prodigies. Funds for education should be spent to improve education for all children. (*utilized*)

J. Self-Assessment Review: Go back to page 113 and reassess your knowledge of the target vocabulary. How has your understanding of the words changed? What words do you feel most comfortable with now?

WRITING AND DISCUSSION TOPICS

1. Interests and abilities seem to run in some families. Is this the result of environmental or hereditary factors? Comment on this using examples from your own experience and from the readings and exercises in this unit.

2. One study of 32 exceptional physics and chemistry students in Taiwan found that the most important factors in the development of their intellectual abilities were family size, family income, and the child's place in the birth order. That is, over 75% of these students were the first-born child in a small family with a relatively high income. Why do you think this is true?

3. Sometimes a child prodigy is raised in a family with other siblings, making it difficult for the parents to maintain a family environment that meets all of the children's needs. What suggestions would you make to such a family to help them create a suitable home environment for all of the children. Consider such factors as family routines, household rules, and discipline.

THE COMPETITIVE INSTINCT

In this unit, you will

- ⮫ read about how competition has shaped business practices through time.
- ⮫ gain familiarity with texts presented in timeline format.
- ⮫ learn how to read timelines and take notes in timeline form.
- ⮫ increase your understanding of the target academic words for this unit:

behalf	commission	currency	license	portion
classic	contract	devote	mechanism	principle
commence	correspond	flexible	parallel	qualitative

SELF-ASSESSMENT OF TARGET WORDS

Think carefully about how well you know each target word in this unit. Then, write it in the appropriate column in the chart.

I have never seen the word before.	I have seen the word but am not sure what it means.	I understand the word when I see or hear it in a sentence.	I have tried to use this word, but I am not sure I am using it correctly.	I use the word with confidence in either speaking *or* writing.	I use the word with confidence, both in speaking *and* writing.

MORE WORDS YOU'LL NEED

instinct: the natural force that causes a person or animal to behave in a certain way without thinking about it.

BEFORE YOU READ

Read these questions. Discuss your answers in a small group.

1. Do you consider yourself to be a competitive person? Why or why not?

2. Do you think the urge to compete is something people are born with or something they learn from their parents? Why?

3. Does society have an effect on an individual's competitive drive? If so, how? Are some societies more competitive than others? Give examples to support your opinions.

READ

This timeline from *BusinessWeek* magazine traces the history of competition—personal, professional, and national.

Personal Best: The Competitive Instinct Timeline

Society is usually the better for the competitive instinct, that raw urge to beat the other guy. Sure, sometimes it can get nasty, but where would mankind be if it didn't? This timeline spotlights some notable moments in the history of personal competition.

Ancient History
Sibling Rivalry
Classical texts—legends, myths, folklore, and religious works—are filled with stories of battles between brothers, between sisters, and even between brothers and sisters. Siblings throughout the ages have rivaled each other for parental attention or approval, power, riches, and love.

476 B.C.E.[1]
Self-Promotion
Wealthy political leader Hiero—winner of the horse race in the 476 B.C.E[1] Olympics—

commissions a laudatory ode[2] from celebrated poet Pindar. Sports marketing is born.

1206
Khan's Conquests
Warlord Genghis Khan unites the tribes of Mongolia under one rule and **commences** a lifelong career of brutal military campaigns. Khan uses his soldiers' competitive instincts to his advantage by basing rewards solely on job performance. He also institutes innovations like coordinated attacks. Khan establishes a **flexible** command structure to control a network of armies in different regions, all fighting on his **behalf**. These armies attack new territory in **parallel** battles and soon sweep across the Asian continent. Khan's armies lay the foundation for the largest contiguous[3] empire in history.

1651
Taming the Beast
Thomas Hobbes publishes *Leviathan*, in which he asserts that man's natural state is anarchic[4] competition. Man is motivated in all things by self-interest. It is this **devotion** to self-interest that induces man to form peaceful societies.

[1] *B.C.E.*: "before common era," referring to the time before year 0 of the standard Western calendar
[2] *laudatory ode*: poem that praises the subject
[3] *contiguous*: touching or next to each other
[4] *anarchic*: recognizing no government or leader

Society follows an unspoken, unwritten social **contract**, without which life would be "nasty, brutish, and short."

1789
Father of U.S. Industry
Textile worker Samuel Slater arrives in the United States from England. He soon builds the young nation's first successful cotton mill (using mostly technology stolen from his former employer). This gives birth to the modern U.S. manufacturing age.

1867
Fight of the "Robber Barons"

Industrial giants Jay Gould and Cornelius Vanderbilt begin their battle for control of the Erie Railroad. Vanderbilt buys millions of dollars' worth of stock, but Gould secretly works with others to issue more shares of the stock, diluting Vanderbilt's **portion** of control. Eventually Vanderbilt leaves the fight.
Gould takes Erie into bankruptcy[5] but makes a lot of money for himself—a corporate strategy he invents.

1901
Testing, testing,...
The era of standardized testing begins. The College Board, a not-for-profit examination service in the United States, administers its first entrance exam to college applicants. The SAT (Scholastic Assessment Test) arrives in 1926. The SAT is still the most common **mechanism** that colleges and universities use to assess applicants.

1957
The Space Race
The Soviet Union[6] launches Sputnik, the first spaceship. Laika, a dog traveling aboard

Sputnik 2, becomes the first mammal in space. The United States enters the space race. The space programs of the U.S. and the Soviet Union parallel each other in a race to be the first to reach the moon. Billions of dollars in aerospace research are spent by each. The U.S. reaches the moon first, in 1969.

1960s
Is Competing Bad for Kids?
Dr. Benjamin Spock writes a series of books devoted to teaching parents how to raise children better. He suggests that competition is bad for children. This idea has an enormous influence on many cultures. Even today, some youth soccer games have no winners and some schools do not give letter grades that **correspond** to a child's performance.

1980
Bill Gates v. Gary Kildall

Company executives from IBM schedule a visit with Gary Kildall at his company, Digital Research. They want to **license** his operating system in IBM's new personal computer. According to legend, Kildall decided to take a flight on his private plane instead of meeting with IBM, but he didn't cancel the appointment. The IBM executives came to Digital Research, but Kindall was not there. A young employee named Bill Gates stepped in and offered to let them license his DOS system instead. IBM agreed, and soon Bill Gates and Microsoft were household names. In the technology industry, this event is referred to as "the day Gary went flying."

---

[5] *bankruptcy*: a state in which a company (or person) cannot pay its debts
[6] *The Soviet Union*: a group of countries that formerly existed as a single political body in eastern Europe and northern Asia, led by Russia and including Ukraine, Lithuania, Kazakhstan, and others

1986
"Greed Is Good"
Ivan Boesky, an expert in international **currency** trading, gives a speech at the University of California, Berkeley. He tells students, "I think greed is healthy. You can be greedy and still feel good about yourself." The **principle** that "greed is good" influences business and economic policies for many years. Within months of his speech, Boesky is sent to prison and fined $100 million for illegal stock trading.

1990s
The Legacy of Jack Welch
General Electric CEO Jack Welch establishes a shocking new policy. Every year, he rates the performance of his entire management staff both **qualitatively** and quantitatively. He then fires the bottom 10%. Managers around the world start to sweat as more CEOs adopt this policy for their companies.

2000
Who Survives?
Survivor quickly takes the No. 1 slot in U.S. television ratings, and begins a reality TV craze. The show puts sixteen  people on a remote, undeveloped island where they compete against each other in various physical and mental games. One by one, the participants vote each other off the island. The last person wins a large cash prize. The term "voted off the island" enters the vocabulary of the business world.

READING STRATEGY: Understanding Timelines

Historical information is sometimes presented as a timeline. Timelines are organized in chronological (time) order. They can start with the earliest or first event and move forward to the most recent or last event, or go the opposite direction—from most recent to most distant.

A. Without looking back at the timeline in Reading 1, put these sections into chronological order, from most recent to most distant. Write 1 (most recent) to 8 (most distant). Compare your answers with a partner.

.... 1990s: The Legacy of Jack Welch

..1.. 2000: Who Survives?

.... Ancient History: Sibling Rivalry

.... 1986: "Greed Is Good"

.... 1651: Taming the Beast

.... 1957: The Space Race

.... 1980: Bill Gates v. Gary Kildall

.... 1867: Fight of the "Robber Barons"

Timelines typically present short descriptions of major events, discoveries, or people. They usually do not give detailed information. Because the descriptions are already brief, students can usually summarize the information easily in their notes.

B. Complete these notes on Reading 1. Write the information that corresponds to the dates given. Try to summarize each section as briefly as you can and still record the important facts. Compare your work in a small group.

Ancient history: ....

....

476 B.C.E.: _Olympic winner Hiero commissions poem about self = 1st sports_
marketing.

1206: ....

....

1651: ....

....

1789: ....

....

1867: ....

....

1901: ....

....

1957: ....

....

1960s: _Dr. Spock—books about raising kids, suggests comp. is bad; big influence—_
today some kids' games have no winners, schools don't give letter grades

1980: ....

....

1986: ....

....

1990s: ....

....

2000: ....

....

A. What is your opinion? Circle the answer that best reflects what you think. In some cases, more than one answer may be correct. Discuss your answers with a partner.

1. If you had to, which of these things would you *commission* an artist to create?

   a. A portrait of yourself

   b. A sculpture of a famous person

   c. A drawing of a family member

2. What is the first thing a person should do before *commencing* work on a project or assignment?

   a. Consult with experts in the field

   b. Read relevant material on the issue

   c. Brainstorm their own ideas on the topic

3. Which of these *mechanisms* is most important for the daily life of a household?

   a. A clock

   b. A light switch

   c. A door handle

4. What is the most important thing to do before signing a *contract* with someone?

   a. Read all parts of the contract completely

   b. Ask the other person questions

   c. Consult with a good lawyer

5. If you had to choose someone to act on your *behalf* in an important legal matter, who would you pick?

   a. Your best friend

   b. A family member

   c. A hired representative you don't know personally

6. Which of these things is it best to evaluate *qualitatively*, with description, rather than quantitatively, using numbers or statistics?

   a. Students' performance in school

   b. Production in a factory

   c. A doctor's diagnosis of a patient

B. Read these excerpts from another text on business. For each excerpt, cross out the one word or phrase in parentheses with a different meaning from the other three choices. Compare your answers with a partner.

1. Patagonia, Inc., an outdoor equipment company in California, differs from the (*traditional* / *classical* / *established* / *innovative*) business model because it focuses on saving the environment rather than increasing profits.

2. Many creative workers come to Patagonia because they are interested in working for a company that values its (*consumers* / *morals* / *values* / *principles*) more than its profits.

3. Patagonia also has (*flexible* / *demanding* / *adaptable* / *changeable*) work hours for its employees, who are encouraged to spend a (*majority* / *part* / *portion* / *segment*) of their workday at the beach when conditions are good for surfing.

4. The company sees professional work and outdoor hobbies not as conflicting demands, but as complementary and (*helpful* / *equivalent* / *parallel* / *similar*) activities.

5. The founder and Chairman of Patagonia, Yvon Chouinard, believes that (*devotion* / *attraction* / *commitment* / *dedication*) to recreation encourages innovation in product development.

6. Chouinard believes that the company's success and profitability (*corresponds to* / *is consistent with* / *is greater than* / *is related to*) its devotion to the environment and sustainable business practices.

C. Which of these jobs should require a license? Put a check (✓) next to them. Then, discuss your ideas in a small group. Together, decide which three are the most important to license, and share your ideas with the class.

.... driving a taxi   .... building houses

.... operating a beauty salon   .... practicing law (being a lawyer)

.... selling medicine   .... taking care of pets

.... teaching children   .... selling food to the public

> The adjective *qualitative* refers to an evaluation of something based on how good it is or on observations of different qualities. It can also be used to refer to evaluations based on opinion rather than fact.
>
> *A **qualitative** study of employee satisfaction found that 75% of workers feel less loyalty to their companies now than they did ten years ago.*
>
> Note, the opposite of qualitative is *quantitative*, referring to evaluations using numbers and statistics.

D. Decide whether each item in the chart is a qualitative or quantitative evaluation. Explain your answers.

	Qualitative	Quantitative
1. 98% of customers that use products from the German software company SAP also use Microsoft Office.		
2. Cirque de Soleil's success is due to its unique combination of circus and theater.		
3. 14% of new business is in new markets, which generates 61% of profits.		
4. Heavy equipment seller Caterpillar saw its profits increase by 38%.		
5. People see the grocery store Whole Foods as representative of a healthy, eco-friendly lifestyle.		

E. Read this story about business in China. Then, go back and restate each of the sentences in your notebook using the words in parentheses. Do not change the meanings of the sentences.

1. Recent graduate Sophia Zhu was not faced with the traditional problem of a difficult job search. (*classic*)

    Recent graduate Sophia Zhu was not faced with the classic problem of a finding a good job.

2. Zhu agreed to work for General Electric (GE), although she could have begun her career with almost any company. (*contract, commenced*)

3. Companies in China are so desperate to find well-trained employees that they offer many incentives, including adaptable working hours and education programs that help employees get professional certification. (*flexible, licenses*)

4. Companies don't offer these benefits because of a moral belief that workers should be well treated. (*principle*)

5. Rather, they hope that employees will reward them with loyalty and stay with the company for a long time. (*devotion*)

6. Chinese companies have developed procedures through which younger workers often rise more quickly into leadership positions than young people on similar tracks in the west. (*mechanisms, parallel*)

7. GE and other companies also offer different amounts of money as a reward for work of appropriate value. For example, they might award an employee $100 to take the family out for dinner after completing a project. (*corresponding, currency*)

8. A part of GE's success in attracting and keeping employees is due to immeasurable benefits. It works hard to make employees feel recognized and appreciated. (*portion, qualitative*)

READING 2

BEFORE YOU READ

Read these questions. Discuss your answers in a small group.

1. Think about people's daily lives one hundred years ago. Which skills did people have then that most people today do not have? What skills do you have that someone in the past probably didn't have?

2. Now think about work. What types of skills are needed today that were not needed in the past? Do you think people's work skills today tend to be more general or more specialized than in the past? Why?

3. What do you think is better for society: large corporations, small family businesses, or a mixture of both? Why?

> In Reading 2, notice that *trade* is used in two different ways. One meaning of *trade* refers to a formal process for exchanging goods and services.
>
> *The leaders are meeting to work out a **trade** agreement that will benefit both countries.*
>
> Another meaning of *trade* refers to jobs for which a person needs specialized skills, especially with the hands.
>
> *My grandfather was an upholsterer and taught all his children the **trade** as well.*
>
> As you read, circle or highlight *trade* wherever it occurs in any form. Make sure you understand which meaning applies in each case.

This introduction from a business textbook gives a brief account of the rise of companies and corporations throughout time.

From One to Many: The Rise of the Corporation

For most of human history, "business" was done one to one—people traded goods and services with each other individually, as families, or as small tribal groups. As time went on and
5 societies formed, people began to *specialize*, to devote their time and energy to one type of work. They were farmers, tailors, laborers, soldiers. They exchanged their goods or services for everything else they needed. Regions
10 started to specialize in a few types of goods and services and commenced regular trading with other regions. Societies created currency, which allowed people to sell their work for money and then use that money to buy the work of
15 others. Urban areas grew and business practices expanded. Eventually, several tradespeople joined together to make one larger business enterprise—a company.

In the mid 16th century, the Muscovy
20 Company had a *monopoly* on trade routes from England to Russia—the only way to ship things between England and Russia was to pay Muscovy. In 1555, it became the first joint-stock company. A joint-stock company is one in which
25 investors give money to help a company expand operations. They then receive a portion of the profit that the company makes. The investors own *stock* in the company. Muscovy's success inspired many imitators. Joint-stock companies
30 soon started to multiply. Most of them wanted to control trade routes from Europe to the New World.

In the 1670s, the English East India Co. became the first company to offer many
35 different types of products and services, and to have parallel operations in many countries at the same time—the first *multinational corporation*. It reached the height of its power in the late 17th and early 18th centuries. The
40 East India Co. even became a military force. It occupied nations and created its own currency. It monopolized trade between East and West in tea, opium, and gunpowder.

By the 1870s, many corporations had become
45 strong and powerful. John D. Rockefeller, for example, built the Standard Oil Company into a huge, super-efficient corporation. It dominated the U.S. oil industry. People said that Standard Oil was a monopoly and that this
50 was wrong. Rockefeller defended his company: "We were all in a sinking ship if competition continued." For Rockefeller, monopolies were good. Competition prevented companies from growing large enough to provide certain services
55 society needed. Some public utilities (electricity, water, trash removal) still operate as monopolies. This allows local government to control and monitor the quality of these services on behalf of the people using them.

60 For most businesses, however, Rockefeller's ideas about competition proved to be wrong. In the early part of the 20th century, competition between companies increased. Companies needed to compete with each other to attract
65 customers. This meant that people had more choices about what they bought. Prices went down and quality went up. General Motors (GM) executive Alfred Sloan adopted a policy that corresponded to these changes in the
70 marketplace and people's expectations. He declared in 1924 that his company would have "a car for every purse and purpose." GM would put the customer first, not the company. This "customer-first" principle changed the
75 automotive industry, and made GM one of the most successful businesses in the United States.

As more and more companies expanded into corporations in the 1950s and 60s, people found new ways to make money from successful, and
80 unsuccessful, businesses. In the 1970s, trader Michael Milken started working with "junk

bonds." These were high-risk investments that had the potential to increase many times in value. The possibility of high returns on a small investment induced thousands and thousands of people to buy junk bonds. Milken became rich and famous. Soon, however, most of these high-risk investments failed. Investors lost millions of dollars. In 1989, Milken went to jail for *fraud*, for tricking people into buying something that was actually worthless.

Business in the new millennium is changing yet again. As the number of multinational corporations increases, cultural issues have become more important. Companies must pay attention to cultural trends, governments, and economic situations in dozens of different parts of the world. They must also maintain offices, hire and manage workers, and obey laws in many different countries. Holiday schedules alone can cause big problems.

Finding workers with the right educational background, work experience, and language skills can also be very difficult. And the workers who have all these things are in high demand. Multinational corporations have to attract workers as well as customers. General Electric, for example, invests a lot of time and money in its international workforce. It offers high salaries, but also personalized leadership training, special assignments, and big bonuses.

Multinationalism is not the only reason for the changes in business in the 21st century. With the rise of computers and the Internet, business practices have had to become much more flexible. In the past, corporations were very secretive. Competitors, and even customers, had little information about how a company operated. But computers and the Internet have made it possible for people to educate themselves. They have the information and the ability to take care of many needs on their own.

Corporations needed to find a way to make the Internet useful for their business. So rather than keeping information secret, they did the opposite. Businesses started providing customers with all the information they might want. They started working *with* customers rather than only providing services *for* them. The customer is still there, but the business relationship is different.

Relationships between businesses are changing, too. Many corporations now practice "co-opetition." The principle behind co-opetition is that cooperation is good, even with competitors. Trading information, goods, and services benefits everyone—or, said another way, *a rising tide floats all boats*.

Many new products, from video to financial services, need complex packages of hardware, software, and services. By working together, such as agreeing on the Wi-Fi standard for high-speed wireless, competitors can expand the market so everyone wins. Competitors also buy or license each other's products to improve their own, which increases sales for both companies.

In the past, a product's market was seen as one small pie. Companies competed with each other for more slices of the pie. Now, companies are working together to increase the size of the pie. Companies measure the success of their practices both qualitatively and quantitatively. They measure how much product quality improves and how much more they sell of it. Today's companies hope that, by trading ideas and information with customers and each other, business will improve for everyone.

READING COMPREHENSION

Mark each sentence as *T* (true) or *F* (false) according to the information in Reading 2. Correct each false statement on the line below it.

.... **1.** When people began to specialize, they devoted themselves to many types of work.

....

.... **2.** The use of currency allowed people to sell their work and buy the work of others.

....

.... **3.** In a joint-stock company, investors receive a portion of the company's profits.

....

.... **4.** In the 1670s, the English East India Co. was one of many multinational corporations.

....

.... **5.** Rockefeller believed that monopolies prevented companies from providing services that society needed.

....

.... **6.** GM's policy of "a car for every purse and purpose" corresponded to the changes in society at that time.

....

.... **7.** In the 1980s, investors made millions of dollars on junk bonds.

....

.... **8.** The principle of co-opetition reflects the fact that many products today use parts or services from competing businesses.

....

READING STRATEGY

Read the article on pages 138–139 again. As you read, take notes in timeline form in your notebook. Choose a date that corresponds to the major events discussed. Then, summarize each section, recording only the important information. Compare your work in a small group.

STEP I VOCABULARY ACTIVITIES: Word Level

A. Read this passage about human and animal competition. Complete the sentences with target words from the box.

commences	devote	parallels
commissions	mechanism	principle
corresponds	on behalf of	

Research on animals shows that the drive to compete is instinctual, and that the human drive to make money and succeed in business has (1) .... in the animal world. Rather than fighting over trademarks and patents, for example, rats fight over territory. When one male rat enters another's space, a battle (2) .... , often to the death.

Desire to compete among animals generally (3) .... to the reproductive instinct or a need for food. As humans have evolved, the (4) .... that controls competition in the human brain has transferred the urge to compete to sports, business, and other activities that are not as closely linked to survival. In order to control humans' desire to win, governments have created (5) .... to oversee mergers and prevent monopolies.

The social instinct of humans also affects the competitive drive. Our emotional bonds with others often result in *altruism*, or actions that benefit others more than oneself. Some individuals (6) .... their whole lives to improving work conditions, for example. Others fight injustice (7) .... those who cannot speak for themselves. This altruistic (8) .... helps balance the competitive instinct and drive people toward cooperation.

The word *commission* has two meanings. In one meaning, the verb means "to ask someone to do a piece of work." It can refer to a work of art, a study, or a special project of any sort. A *commission* is the result.

> They **commissioned** a study to gather evidence on how computer usage affects arm muscles.

> She received the **commission** to paint the CEO's portrait.

A *commission* can also refer to a group of people who are given official responsibility to regulate or investigate something. A *commissioner* is the leader of a commission.

> The Competition **Commission** is a British governmental organization that monitors British companies to make sure they are competing fairly.

B. With a partner, look at these commissions and discuss them. What might each commission regulate or investigate? Is a commission necessary to regulate these areas? Why or why not?

1. Commission on Human Rights
2. Parks and Recreation Commission
3. International Trade Commission
4. Commission on Ocean Policy
5. Atomic Energy Commission
6. Fish and Wildlife Commission

The word *currency* usually refers to different types of money. It can also refer to anything that is acting as a mechanism for exchange, or for anything that has abstract value in a certain situation.

> You can trade euros for yen at the **currency** exchange office.   (type of money)

> In the Internet world, information is the most valuable **currency**.   (something of value)

> Managers resisted the new hiring policy at first, but it has gained **currency** lately. Now, they agree it's the best system.   (abstract value)

C. In what situations might these things be used as currency? Use your imagination and think of one or two situations for each. Discuss your ideas in a small group.

1. information
2. airplane tickets
3. a car
4. the ability to speak another language
5. silence
6. a cell phone

STEP II VOCABULARY ACTIVITIES: Sentence Level

D. Read the story about sports and management. Then, go back and restate each of the sentences in your notebook using the words in parentheses as indicated. Do not change the meanings of the sentences.

1. Theories of business management are being applied to other areas with great success. (*principles*)

   Principles of business management are being successfully applied to other areas.

2. In Maryland, the coach of the Terrapins' soccer team had been following a traditional model of team leadership by making his best players into team captains. Unfortunately, their leadership ability did not equal their sports skills. (*classic, correspond*)

3. The coach, Sasho Cirovski, saw similarities between what he needed and his brother Vancho's work in human resources. He decided to begin the next practice with a survey that Vancho used for organizational development. (*parallels, commence*)

4. The survey asked team members to associate descriptive characteristics with individuals on the team, for example, by identifying those who helped them increase their commitment to the team. (*qualitative, devotion*)

5. Based on the results of the survey, Coach Cirovski discovered that a player he had not seen as a leader, Scott Buete, had the respect of the team. Cirovski decided that he should be more adaptable in his selection of team leaders. He made an agreement with Buete that he would become a third team captain. (*flexible, contract*)

6. For the remaining part of the season, the team played much better. It seemed that Cirovski had finally found the right system for choosing a leader. (*portion, mechanism*)

Devotion refers to commitment, love, or dedication. If people are *devoted* to something, they are committed to it. If they are *devoted* to someone, that usually means that they love that person.

   A good soccer player should be **devoted** to her team.

To *devote time to* or *devote money to* something is another way of saying *spend time on* or *spend money on* something.

   A good player **devotes** <u>a lot of time and energy</u> to practice.

E. Restate these sentences to include *devote*. Use each form at least once in your sentences. Compare your sentences with a partner.

1. Businesses used to expect a strong commitment from their employees.

2. Nowadays, employees are rarely so attached to their company that they stay longer than a few years.

continued

3. Many employees leave companies because they are expected to spend a lot of time on work-related projects.

4. They believe that companies should not expect employees to be loyal when they are asked to do an increasing amount of work.

5. At first, some businesses spent more money to try to get employees to stay with the company.

6. Now, however, most businesses have decided that they can't afford to buy the affection of their employees.

7. Instead of expecting company loyalty, they now expect employees to leave after a certain time and to get a regular number of new employees.

F. What do you think is important in a business manager? Rank these qualities from *1* (most important) to *8* (least important). Then, write a paragraph in which you explain your ranking. Be prepared to read aloud or discuss your ideas with the class.

.... highly principled

.... devoted to employees

.... devoted to company

.... well paid in relation to other employees

.... honest

.... flexible

.... focused on classic, time-honored strategies

.... innovative thinker

G. Self-Assessment Review: Go back to page 129 and reassess your knowledge of the target vocabulary. How has your understanding of the words changed? What words do you feel most comfortable with now?

WRITING AND DISCUSSION TOPICS

1. Which do you think is a stronger instinct, cooperation or competition? Explain your answer with personal experience and ideas and examples from this unit.

2. What do you think is better for business, employees who stay at one company for a long time, or employees who work at many companies over their lifetimes? Why?

3. Is it better to evaluate employees qualitatively (for example, by describing their work style, accomplishments, etc.) or quantitatively (for example, by assigning them a number that reflects their skills and abilities)?

4. Look at these two metaphors from Reading 2:

   "We were all in a sinking ship if competition continued."

   "A rising tide floats all boats."

   Explain what you think each metaphor means. Then, decide which one you agree with. Explain your choice with personal experience and ideas and examples from this unit.

GETTING THERE

In this unit, you will

⊃ read about the latest developments in global navigation.

⊃ identify and discuss metaphors.

⊃ utilize online encyclopedias.

⊃ increase your understanding of the target academic words for this unit:

assemble	crucial	incidence	precise	target
attribute	enable	item	prohibit	vary
chart	equivalent	manual	significant	

SELF-ASSESSMENT OF TARGET WORDS

Think carefully about how well you know each target word in this unit. Then, write it in the appropriate column in the chart.

I have never seen the word before.	I have seen the word but am not sure what it means.	I understand the word when I see or hear it in a sentence.	I have tried to use the word, but I am not sure I am using it correctly.	I use the word with confidence in either speaking *or* writing.	I use the word with confidence, both in speaking *and* writing.

MORE WORDS YOU'LL NEED

cartography: the science or art of making maps

cartographer: one who makes maps

G.P.S.: Global Positioning System: a navigational system using satellites to identify locations

navigate: to decide on and steer a course, to make one's way over or through something

BEFORE YOU READ

Read these questions. Discuss your answers in a small group.

1. How did you learn to get around on your own in your city? When did you first go somewhere without an adult to lead the way? Where did you go? How did you find your way?

2. What's the hardest thing about finding your way around a new city? In a new place, do you find it more difficult to drive or take mass transit? Why?

3. Are you good at reading maps? Give an example to support your answer. Would you like to have a device that showed you or told you where to go each step of the way? Why or why not?

READING STRATEGY: Identifying and Understanding Metaphors

A *metaphor* is a descriptive expression. It is a word or phrase from another context that replaces a more ordinary word or phrase in a text. This change of context suggests a comparison of the two things. Metaphors are more symbolic than direct comparisons and usually evoke an image for the reader.

> *The cow stood grazing alongside <u>the lunar landscape of potholes</u> that formed the only road in the region.*

By calling the road a "lunar landscape," the writer evokes an image of the surface of the moon. This comparison helps the reader imagine the appearance and condition of the road.

As you read, notice the metaphors the author uses. They have been underlined for your reference.

READ

This excerpt from an article in *The New Yorker* magazine gives insight into how Internet maps are created and maintained.

GETTING THERE: THE SCIENCE OF DRIVING DIRECTIONS
BY NICK PAUMGARTEN

In the fifteenth century, Henry the Navigator, a Portuguese prince, presided over a court in Sagres that became a center for cartographers, instrument-makers, and explorers, whose 5 expeditions he sponsored. Seafarers returning to Sagres from the west coast of Africa reported their discoveries, and new maps were produced, extending the reaches of the known world. These maps became very valuable, owing to their utility 10 in trade, war, and religious expansion, and were jealously guarded as state secrets.

Today's **equivalent** is a company called Navteq. It is the leading provider of geographic data to the Internet mapping sites and the personal-navigation industry—<u>the boiler room of the where-you-are-and-what-to-do business</u>. Its only real competitor is a Belgian company called Tele Atlas. Most of the websites, car manufacturers, and gizmo[1]-makers—anyone involved in what are known as intelligent transportation systems—get the bulk of their raw material from these two companies. The clients differ mainly in how they choose to present the data. This allows civilians[2] to have preferences.

The G.P.S. city

Despite the digitization of maps and the satellites circling the earth, the cartographic revolution still relies heavily on fresh observations made by people. Navteq, like Prince Henry, produces updates periodically (usually four times a year) for its corporate clients. Its explorers are its geographic analysts. These people go onto the roads to make sure everything that the satellite data says about those roads is true—to check the old routes and record the new ones. The practice is called ground-truthing. They drive around and take note of what they call "**attributes**," anything of **significance** to a traveler seeking his way. A road segment can have a hundred and sixty attributes, everything from a speed limit to a drawbridge, an on-ramp[3], or a **prohibition** against U-turns[4]. New signs, new roads, new exits, new rules: if such alterations go uncollected by Navteq, the traveler, relying on a device or a map produced by one of Navteq's clients, might well get lost or confused. A driver making a simple left turn can encounter <u>a blizzard of attributes</u>: one-way, speed limit, crosswalk, traffic light, street sign, turn restriction, two-way, hydrant.

Navteq has about six hundred field researchers and offices in twenty-three countries. There are nine field researchers in the New York metropolitan area. One morning this fall, I went out with a pair of them, Chris Arcari and Shovie Singh. "We're going to be working over by LaGuardia Airport," Arcari said. "One of the **items** we need to check out is some street names. They've put up new signs. Then we'll proceed to an area that we have **targeted**." Arcari, who is thirty-seven and was brought up on Long Island, was the senior member of the team, and he tended to speak in the formal, euphemistic[5] manner of a police officer testifying in court. He'd been with Navteq for ten years. Singh, a native of Trinidad who grew up in Queens, New York, was a new hire. He'd got hooked on geography after taking some classes in the subject in college.

They were, you might say, free-driving—no navigation device or map—because they are not only locals but also professionals in the New York-area discipline of getting from here to there. They spend two to three days a week just driving around. Manhattan's grid may be the easiest road network to master in the developed world (if we overlook some areas), yet the routes leading to and from it are as tricky as the

---

[1] *gizmo*: any small mechanical or electronic device, gadget
[2] *civilian*: any person not connected with a particular area of interest
[3] *on-ramp*: the approach to a highway
[4] *U-turn*: a turn that takes a driver in the opposite direction
[5] *euphemistic*: formal or polite, rather than casual and direct

tributaries[6] of the Amazon. The highways are <u>a mad thatch of interstates, parkways, boulevards, and spurs</u>, plus river crossings galore, each with its own virtues and idiosyncrasies[7]. There are many ways to get from point A to point B in New York, and, because of all the variations, anyone can be a route-selection expert, or at least an enthusiast. Family gatherings inevitably feature relatives eating cocktail nuts and arguing over the merits of various exits and shortcuts.

Eventually, we pulled into a gas station near the airport. Singh and Arcari **assembled** their equipment. They mounted a G.P.S. antenna, shaped like a giant mushroom, on the roof of the car. The antenna was connected to a laptop, upon which a map would show our progress—a G.P.S. track. Singh took the wheel. Arcari sat in back with the laptop, ready to note any changes.

The first thing the men noticed was a "No Left Turn" sign out of the gas station. "That doesn't go in the database," Arcari said. "That's unofficial, since it pertains to a private enterprise."

An analyst has some leeway in proposing research missions in his territory. "The situation at LaGuardia was something I had noticed myself and thought should be revisited," Arcari explained. In his free time, he'd been driving past the airport and, nudged by curiosity, if not conscience, had made a little detour. He discovered that the Port Authority of New York and New Jersey, which runs the airport, had put up a few new road signs. This was the situation at LaGuardia.

"We'll circle around the perimeter and then check the terminals," Arcari said. "As we're driving, I'm checking our information against what exists in reality." Left on Runway Drive ("drop a name check"), merge onto LaGuardia Road (another name check), left onto Delta Arrivals Road. The sign for it was new. "A valid unnamed feature," Arcari said, turning the laptop so that I could follow along as he

recorded it onscreen. "I point an arrow to where the feature occurred."

Seeing the road through the eyes of a ground-truther made it seem <u>a thicket of signage</u>—commands and designations vying for attention, like a nightmare you might have after a day of studying for a driving exam. Once you start looking for attributes, you spot them everywhere.

"Why don't we loop around again?" Arcari said. "I want to be sure we collected everything correctly."

The familiar frustration of going around and around on an airport road was compensated for by the fact that no one was lost or late. After the extra <u>orbit</u>, we drove into Astoria, the neighborhood next to the airport. Arcari approached the neighborhood by driving around the outside of the "project area," and then going up and down the streets within it. He observed that, driving around like this, you become acutely aware of how many people are not at work. Arcari said that one of the issues that has come up in New York in recent years is the naming of streets and squares for the victims of the attacks on September 11, 2001. We came upon one of them, James Marcel Cartier Way, and Arcari was pleased to see that the name was in the database. A kind of contentment took hold, as other anomalies encountered along the way—an unlikely median strip, a "Do Not Enter" sign—turned out to be accounted for.

Over lunch at a local diner, we discussed various attribute **incidents**. "One item that was an issue: on the Brooklyn-Queens Expressway, they started renumbering the exits. They did some but didn't do others, so for a while there were two Exit 41s."

After lunch, Arcari and Singh were due back at the central office, in Syosset, to download their findings. They offered to drive me back into Manhattan, but we agreed that it would

---

[6] *tributary*: a stream that feeds a larger stream or river
[7] *idiosyncrasy*: particular characteristic

make more sense for me to take the subway. None of us knew where to find it, though. Subway stations are not attributes; Navteq 165 honors the automobile, a trend started by the makers of road maps of a century ago, whose

mandate was to promote auto travel and, with it, the purchase of gasoline, cars, and tires. We pulled into a gas station, and I ran inside to ask 170 for directions.

READING STRATEGY

A. Think about the metaphors in Reading 1 and answer the questions. Compare answers with a partner.

1. Line 15

   What is a *boiler room*? What does it mean to be "the boiler room" for an entire business?

2. Line 47

   What is a *blizzard*? Why does the writer choose this word to make his point?

3. Line 79

   What is a *thatch*? What does *mad* mean here? What is the author trying to communicate with this metaphor?

4. Line 123

   What is a *thicket*? Which other metaphor above is this one very similar to? What does it mean to *see something through someone else's eyes*?

5. Line 135

   What is an *orbit*? What image does this word suggest? Why does the writer use it in this context?

B. With a partner, read these metaphors and discuss them. Think of a context in which a writer might use them effectively. Share your ideas in a small group.

1. a sea of troubles: ....

2. a web of deceit: ....

3. a trail of lies: ....

4. a veil of secrecy: ....

5. a labyrinth of hallways: ....

An *attribute* is a quality or feature of someone or something.

> *They drive around and take note of what they call "**attributes**," anything of significance to a traveler seeking his way.*

The verb *attribute* means "to believe that something was caused or done by something or someone." It takes the preposition *to*. It can be used in active or passive form.

Active: *He **attributed** his poor performance on the driving test **to** lack of sleep the night before.*

Passive: *The fault for the accident **was attributed to** the driver of the other car.*

Pronunciation note: In the noun form, the stress is on the first syllable. In the verb form, the stress is on the second syllable.

A. Complete these sentences with the active or passive form of *attribute*. Be sure to use the correct tense. Read your completed sentences aloud to a partner, paying attention to pronunciation.

1. The guide .... his excellent sense of direction to the years he spent with his grandfather, hunting and trapping in the woods.

2. The power failure on the east side of town .... to the recent storms and high winds.

3. The map of the Texas interior .... to Alonso de Santa Cruz.

4. He .... her confidence on the road to the years she spent driving an ambulance in the city.

B. Put a check (✓) next to the things you think would be considered attributes by the ground-truthers in Reading 1. Discuss your answers in a small group.

.... **1.** a stop sign

.... **2.** an animal crossing area

.... **3.** a mall's parking garage

.... **4.** an automotive supply store

.... **5.** a gas station

.... **6.** a bus stop

.... **7.** the poor condition of a major road

.... **8.** a highway rest area

STEP II VOCABULARY ACTIVITIES: Sentence Level

Word Form Chart			
Noun	Verb	Adjective	Adverb
incident incidence	....	incidental	incidentally

The noun *incidence* generally refers to the number of times something (usually something bad) happens.

*There is a high **incidence** of traffic accidents during the first snowfall of the year.*

The noun *incident* refers to a particular event, usually involving violence, danger, or something strange.

*There were two **incidents** of fighting among the fans at the football game.*

The adjective *incidental* refers to minor events that accompany something bigger.

*Despite some **incidental** problems during construction, the building was completed on schedule.*

The adverb *incidentally* is often used to change the subject, usually to something related but not very important. It has the same meaning as *by the way*.

*The mall was really crowded today, but I was able to find that sweatshirt for Peter. **Incidentally**, the travel bookstore you like isn't there anymore. It moved downtown.*

C. In your notebook, restate each of these statements using a form of *incidence*. Use each form at least once.

1. In the general population, the rate of traffic accidents decreases in proportion to the age of the driver.

2. The new Impressa has the highest safety rating of any car in its class from three major car-rating organizations—and it's the car that a lot of rappers drive.

3. The report on the radio said that there was a minor conflict at the soccer game last night, which caused the game to start a few minutes late.

4. Before the guide started the tour of the presidential palace, she gave us some trivia about the buildings in the neighborhood.

D. Circle the item that best completes each statement. In your notebook, write a few sentences explaining your choice. Be prepared to read your sentences aloud or discuss your ideas with the class.

1. For me, the closest equivalent to reading a book is...

   a. taking a nap.   c. studying.

   b. watching a movie.   d. listening to someone tell a story.

2. For me, the closest equivalent to playing with a small child is...

   a. writing an imaginative story.   c. conducting a sociological experiment.

   b. playing a sport.   d. watching a funny movie.

3. For me, the closest equivalent to an evening at the opera is...

   a. a visit to an art museum.   c. a visit to the home of a relative I
                                           don't like.
   b. a visit to the home of a relative
      I like.   d. going to a movie.

READING 2

BEFORE YOU READ

Read these questions. Discuss your answers in a small group.

1. What is the difference between a dictionary and an encyclopedia? How is each one usually used?

2. What attributes might an online encyclopedia have that a printed book could not have?

3. If you were asked to write an encyclopedia entry on any subject, what would you choose? What types of information would you include? What would you exclude? What resources would you consult?

There are many encyclopedias on the Internet. One, however, approaches the task of gathering information differently from the others. While traditional encyclopedias hire researchers and writers to supply their content, Wikipedia (www.wikipedia.org) relies on its *users*. Anyone can write, edit, and update the entries on the website.

Caution: Whenever you use Wikipedia for an academic paper, be sure to cite it as carefully as you would cite any other reference source. Be advised that some instructors will not accept Wikipedia as a reference source for an academic paper, so check with your instructor before using it.

This encyclopedia entry from Wikipedia addresses navigation in the sense of determining position and direction on or above the surface of the Earth.

Navigation

Methods

There are several different branches of navigation, including but not limited to:

- Celestial navigation—navigating by observing the sun, moon, stars, and sometimes planets.
- Pilotage—using visible natural and man-made features such as sea marks and beacons.
- Dead reckoning—using course and speed to determine position.
- Off-course navigation—deliberately aiming to one side of the destination to allow for **variability** in the heading.
- Electronic navigation—using electronic equipment such as radios and satellite navigation systems to follow a course. Also Electronic **Chart** Display and Information System.
- Position fixing—determining current position by visual and electronic means.
- Collision avoidance using radar.

History

The earliest form of navigation was land navigation. This relied on physical landmarks to chart the journey from one place to another. Marine navigation began when prehistoric man attempted to guide his vessel, perhaps a log, across the water using familiar coastal landmarks. Dead reckoning was probably next. It was used to navigate when landmarks were out of sight. Ancient sailors used celestial bodies to steer by, but celestial navigation as known today was not used until people better understood the motion of the sun and stars. Nautical charts were developed to record new navigational and piloting information for other navigators. The development of accurate celestial navigation allowed ships to better determine position.

The most important instrument for nautical navigation was the navigator's diary. These diaries contained **crucial** information. They often became trade secrets because they **enabled** safe travel to profitable ports. Some time later, around the year 300, the magnetic compass was invented in China. This let sailors continue sailing a course even when the weather limited the sky's visibility.

After Isaac Newton published the *Principia*, navigation was transformed. Starting in 1670, the entire world was measured using essentially modern latitude instruments and the best available clocks. In 1730, the sextant was invented. A sextant uses mirrors to measure the altitude of celestial objects in relation to the horizon.

In the late 19th century, Nikola Tesla invented radio. Soon, radio beacons and radio direction finders were providing accurate land-based fixes[1] even hundreds of miles from shore. This system lasted until modern satellite navigation systems made it obsolete.

Around 1960, LORAN was developed. This measured how long a radio wave took to travel between antennas at known locations to fix positions. The equipment could then locate geographic positions to within a half mile (800 m). At about the same, TRANSIT, the first satellite-based navigation system, was developed. It was the first electronic navigation system to provide global coverage.

In 1974, the first GPS satellite was launched. GPS systems now give accurate locations with an error of only a few meters. They also have **precision** timing to less than a microsecond. GLONASS is a positioning system that was launched by the Soviet Union. It relies on a slightly different model of the Earth. Galileo is a competing system that will be placed into service by the European Union.

Polynesian navigation

In the pre-modern history of human migration and nautical exploration, a few peoples have excelled as seafarers. Prominent examples include the Polynesians and the Micronesians of the Pacific Ocean.

The Polynesian navigators routinely crossed thousands of miles of open ocean to reach tiny islands. They used only their own senses and knowledge passed down from generation to generation. In Eastern Polynesia, navigators memorized

---

[1] *fix*: a determination of one's position

extensive catalogs of information in order to help them navigate at various times of day throughout the year. These catalogs included information about:

- the motion of specific stars, and where they would rise and set on the horizon of the ocean.
- the weather.
- time of travel.
- wildlife species (some of which assembled at particular locations).
- ocean swells, and how they would affect the crew.
- the color of the sea and sky, especially how certain types of clouds would assemble at particular locations above some islands.
- the angle at which they should approach a harbor.

These sets of information were kept as *guild secrets*. Generally, each island maintained a guild, or group, of master navigators who had very high status. In times of famine or difficulty, only they could trade for aid or evacuate people. The guild secrets were almost lost. Fortunately, one of the last living navigators taught them to a professional small boat captain so that he could write them down in book form.

Sources

- Admiralty (British Navy) **Manual** of Seamanship, ISBN 0-11-772696-6
- American Practical Navigator

External links

- Local Positioning Systems for Navigation—Complimentary and Alternative Positioning Technologies to GPS
- LBS Insight   News site on wireless navigation services
- Navigation   U.S Army Manual.
- Celestial Navigation
- Bowditch Online   complete online edition of Nathaniel Bowditch's *American Practical Navigator*

READING COMPREHENSION

Mark each sentence as *T* (true) or *F* (false) according to the information in Reading 2. Use the dictionary to help you understand new words.

.... **1.** Sailors using the method of celestial navigation might occasionally rely on the position of other planets for guidance.

.... **2.** The most important item in the ancient navigator's toolbox was his diary.

.... **3.** The sextant helped sailors more accurately determine their positions based on measuring the positions of the stars.

.... **4.** The magnetic compass was recently invented by the European Union.

.... **5.** Radio beacons and direction finders became obsolete after the invention of satellite navigation systems.

.... **6.** Ancient Polynesian navigators crossed the open ocean with the aid of sophisticated clocks.

.... **7.** Polynesian navigational knowledge passed down by oral tradition was finally written in book form.

.... **8.** There are various navigation and positioning systems about which Wikipedia can provide information.

STEP I VOCABULARY ACTIVITIES: Word Level

A *chart* can take many forms. It can be a table, a graph, a diagram, or any graphic representation of information—for example, a Word Form Chart used in this book.

A. Match the picture of each chart with its type, listed in the box. Compare answers with a partner and discuss the function of each type of chart.

a. eye chart	**c.** flow chart	**e.** pie chart
b. flip chart	**d.** medical chart	**f.** sales chart

.... 1.

.... 2.

.... 3.

.... 4.

.... 5.

.... 6.

The word *precise* is an adjective meaning "clear and accurate; giving a lot of detail." The adverb form is *precisely* and has a similar meaning to *exactly*.

The noun form, *precision*, means "the quality of being clear or exact." *Precision* can also be used as an adjective to describe something that has precision.

*Each and every component was manufactured with great **precision**.*

*To work on a high-**precision** vehicle, the mechanic must use **precision** tools.*

B. In your opinion, which of these items require precision? Put a check (✓) next to them. Why do you think it is crucial for them to be precise? Discuss your answers in a small group.

.... **1.** measurements for new carpeting

.... **2.** the time you agree to meet a friend

.... **3.** a portrait (a painting of someone)

.... **4.** a history book

.... **5.** the fit of your clothes

.... **6.** a legal agreement between two friends

.... **7.** the position of items on your desk

.... **8.** instructions to an experienced babysitter

Vary has many members in its word family. Here are example sentences to illustrate some of the more common ones. Check your dictionary for exact definitions.

Nouns

variety	*Ancient travelers used a **variety** of landmarks to navigate their way.*
variation	*Most coastal cultures developed the canoe, but there are many **variations** in its design.*
variance	*His conclusions were totally at **variance** with the evidence.*
variable	*New car designers consider **variables** like where it will be driven, weather conditions, and how many passengers it might carry.*

Adjectives

various	*There are **various** routes you can take to get to work, but this is the fastest.*
variable	*Be careful driving here at night. Road conditions are **variable** and sometimes dangerous.*

C. Complete these sentences using a form of *vary*.

1. Some people .... their routes depending on the day and time.

2. Engine temperature is the most important .... to pay attention to when driving in the desert.

continued

3. He decided to move to California for .... reasons.

4. Reports from the different field offices were at .... with our expectations.

5. The G.P.S. system in the rental car had a wide .... of options for customizing our itinerary.

6. Researchers have found wide .... in driving ability among people of .... ages.

7. In this area, bears have been .... spotted in wooded areas, residential neighborhoods, and parking lots behind buildings.

8. In springtime, the weather is usually more .... than in summer.

D. Complete the sentences about another type of navigational system using the target vocabulary in the box. Use each item one time. Compare answers with a partner.

assemble	enable	precisely
attribute	equivalent	prohibit
chart	items	significant
crucial	manual	

1. The Aboriginal people of Australia had a system of songs, called the Songlines. These songs identified landmarks and other .... (plants, rocks,
(things)
waterholes) useful in finding one's way through the desert.

2. The Songlines were .... to a continental navigational
(identical)
.... , or a kind of Australian travel ....
(map) *(instruction book)*

3. In addition to describing the physical .... of each
(characteristics)
.... landmark, the songs also often explained how the landmarks
(important)
were created and named.

4. Aboriginals used this labyrinth of pathways to .... for rituals, to
(come together)
.... or .... travel across territorial boundaries, or
(allow) *(not allow)*
to hunt for food and water.

5. To work well as a navigational system, it was .... that the songs
(extremely important)
be sung in the appropriate order and that each song be sung ....
(exactly right)

STEP II VOCABULARY ACTIVITIES: Sentence Level

As an adjective or adverb, *manual* or *manually* means "done by the hands."

*Building a road requires a lot of machines, but also a lot of **manual** labor.*

*When the power went out, we had to do everything **manually**.*

As a noun, a *manual* is a book that explains how to do or operate something.

*I can't figure out how to fix this. I need a **manual**.*

E. In your notebook, write a short description of these items. Explain who might use each one and for what purpose. Discuss your ideas with a partner.

1. an owner's (or user's) manual

2. a style manual

3. a computer manual

4. a wilderness survival manual

5. a camera manual

Crucial can be used as a simple adjective before the noun, as in a *crucial decision*. To make the meaning stronger or more dramatic, use an "it" structure.

*It is **crucial** that she get to the hospital within the hour.*

Notice the grammar in the above sentence: . . . *crucial that she get* . . . . This grammar is common in sentences with "it" structures that stress importance or urgency.

It's important that he know the truth.

It is vital that it get finished today.

F. Write one or more answers for each of these questions. Discuss your answers in a small group. Decide which of your ideas is the most crucial in each case. Discuss your choices with the class.

1. What is a crucial problem for humanity?

....

2. What was a crucial moment in history?

....

3. What is a crucial decision you must make for your future?

....

G. Read these situations. In your notebook, explain what must be done in each case, using the word in parentheses. Try to use the grammar noted in the box above. Be prepared to read your sentences aloud or discuss them with the class.

1. You have a test in the morning that will make up 50% of your grade. (*crucial*)

2. You have gotten three speeding tickets this year. If you get one more, your license will be taken away. (*important*)

continued

3. Your elderly grandmother is arriving on a plane at 2:00, but you have to work until 3:00. Your friend has volunteered to pick her up for you. (*essential*)

4. You found exactly the car you want after months of looking. Three other people want it, too. The owner has promised it to you, if you give her the money for it today. (*vital*)

5. Your little nephew's birthday party is tomorrow morning. You bought him a special toy he has wanted for a long time, and now you have to assemble it. It has many small parts and a ten-page instruction manual. (*necessary*)

H. Self-Assessment Review: Go back to page 145 and reassess your knowledge of the target vocabulary. How has your understanding of the words changed? What words do you feel most comfortable with now?

WRITING AND DISCUSSION TOPICS

1. Plan a trip around the world. From your city, make precisely ten stops before you return. In charting your course, try to make the most efficient use of time and money. How long will the trip take? How will you get from city to city? What will you do in each place? How will you get around?

2. What predictions would you make for the future of navigation? Have we advanced as far as we can in this field? Is there anything missing that you would like to see someday?

3. Think carefully about all the navigational attributes you rely on in your daily travels for school, work, shopping, or socializing. Which of these attributes do you consider to be the most crucial?

4. G.P.S. is often used for tracking wild animals. How do you suppose this works? What kind of information might it provide? Of what value is this?

5. There are several gender stereotypes associated with navigation. For example, men don't like to ask for directions, or women don't like to use maps. In your experience, is there any truth to these generalizations? Why do you say so? How do you explain these stereotypes?

Inside Reading 3

The Academic Word List
(words targeted in Level 3 are bold)

Word	Sublist	Location	Word	Sublist	Location	Word	Sublist	Location
abandon	8	L1, U7	attain	9	L1, U5	complex	2	L4, U2
abstract	**6**	**L3, U5**	**attitude**	**4**	**L4, U6**	component	3	L4, U3
academy	**5**	**L3, U1**	attribute	4	L3, U10	compound	5	L4, U6
access	4	L1, U2	author	6	L2, U4	comprehensive	7	L2, U7
accommodate	9	L2, U7	authority	1	L1, U6	comprise	7	L4, U9
accompany	8	L1, U2	**automate**	**8**	**L3, U6**	compute	2	L4, U8
accumulate	8	L2, U4	**available**	**1**	**L3, U5**	conceive	10	L4, U10
accurate	6	L4, U6	aware	5	L1, U5	**concentrate**	**4**	**L3, U8**
achieve	2	L4, U1				**concept**	**1**	**L3, U1**
acknowledge	6	L1, U7	**behalf**	**9**	**L3, U9**	conclude	2	L1, U6
acquire	2	L1, U4	benefit	1	L4, U2	concurrent	9	L4, U5
adapt	7	L4, U7	bias	8	L4, U8	conduct	2	L1, U9
adequate	4	L2, U4	bond	6	L4, U3	confer	4	L4, U4
adjacent	10	L2, U3	**brief**	**6**	**L3, U6**	confine	9	L1, U10
adjust	5	L4, U3	bulk	9	L4, U9	confirm	7	L4, U10
administrate	2	L1, U3				conflict	5	L1, U2
adult	**7**	**L3, U6**	capable	6	L1, U8	conform	8	L4, U7
advocate	7	L1, U10	capacity	5	L4, U9	consent	3	L4, U7
affect	2	L2, U6	category	2	L4, U5	consequent	2	L2, U3
aggregate	6	L1, U9	cease	9	L4, U10	**considerable**	**3**	**L3, U8**
aid	7	L2, U7	**challenge**	**5**	**L3, U8**	consist	1	L4, U2, U9
albeit	10	L1, U7	channel	7	L1, U3	constant	3	L4, U8
allocate	6	L2, U6	**chapter**	**2**	**L3, U7**	constitute	1	L1, U4
alter	5	L1, U1	**chart**	**8**	**L3, U10**	constrain	3	L1, U8
alternative	3	L1, U10	chemical	7	L2, U10	**construct**	**2**	**L3, U1**
ambiguous	8	L1, U4	circumstance	3	L2, U10	consult	5	L1, U6
amend	5	L2, U9	cite	6	L4, U10	consume	2	L2, U2
analogy	9	L1, U4	civil	4	L1, U4	contact	5	L2, U10
analyze	1	L2, U3	clarify	8	L4, U8	contemporary	8	L1, U7
annual	4	L1, U9	**classic**	**7**	**L3, U9**	context	1	L1, U4
anticipate	9	L2, U3	clause	5	L2, U8	**contract**	**1**	**L3, U9**
apparent	4	L2, U9	code	4	L4, U9	contradict	8	L2, U2
append	8	L2, U10	coherent	9	L2, U5	contrary	7	L1, U6
appreciate	**8**	**L3, U5**	coincide	9	L1, U5	contrast	4	L1, U7
approach	**1**	**L3, U1**	collapse	10	L4, U10	contribute	3	L1, U9
appropriate	2	L1, U8	colleague	10	L1, U5	controversy	9	L2, U3
approximate	**4**	**L3, U4**	**commence**	**9**	**L3, U9**	convene	3	L1, U4
arbitrary	8	L2, U8	**comment**	**3**	**L3, U3**	converse	9	L2, U8
area	1	L4, U1	**commission**	**2**	**L3, U9**	convert	7	L2, U2
aspect	**2**	**L3, U4**	commit	4	L2, U6	convince	10	L1, U3
assemble	**10**	**L3, U10**	commodity	8	L4, U6	cooperate	6	L1, U2
assess	1	L1, U8	**communicate**	**4**	**L3, U2**	coordinate	3	L2, U6
assign	6	L2, U9	community	2	L2, U7	core	3	L2, U5
assist	2	L2, U5	compatible	9	L1, U9	corporate	3	L2, U2
assume	1	L2, U1	**compensate**	**3**	**L3, U4**	**correspond**	**3**	**L3, U9**
assure	**9**	**L3, U4**	compile	10	L2, U6	**couple**	**7**	**L3, U1**
attach	**6**	**L3, U7**	complement	8	L1, U7	create	1	L2, U1

Word	Sublist	Location	Word	Sublist	Location	Word	Sublist	Location
credit	2	**L3, U6**	**enable**	5	**L3, U10**	**function**	1	**L3, U1**
criteria	3	**L3, U3**	**encounter**	10	**L3, U5**	**fund**	3	**L3, U3**
crucial	8	**L3, U10**	energy	5	L2, U5	fundamental	5	L4, U4
culture	2	L4, U10	enforce	5	L4, U7	furthermore	6	L4, U9
currency	8	**L3, U9**	**enhance**	6	**L3, U1**			
cycle	4	L4, U5	**enormous**	10	**L3, U8**	gender	6	L2, U8
			ensure	3	L2, U5	generate	5	L1, U5
data	1	L2, U3	entity	5	L4, U5	generation	5	L1, U7
debate	4	L2, U4	**environment**	1	**L3, U8**	**globe**	7	**L3, U2**
decade	7	L1, U7	equate	2	L2, U2	**goal**	4	**L3, U3**
decline	5	L1, U2	equip	7	L2, U3	grade	7	L1, U7
deduce	3	L4, U7	**equivalent**	5	**L3, U10**	grant	4	L2, U9
define	1	**L3, U2**	erode	9	L1, U9	guarantee	7	L2, U8
definite	7	**L3, U4**	error	4	L1, U10	**guideline**	8	**L3, U3**
demonstrate	3	L1, U5	establish	1	L1, U6			
denote	8	L4, U6	estate	6	L4, U6	**hence**	4	**L3, U5**
deny	7	L4, U10	estimate	1	L2, U10	**hierarchy**	7	**L3, U4**
depress	10	L2, U4	ethic	9	L2, U9	highlight	8	L4, U3
derive	1	L4, U10	**ethnic**	4	**L3, U3**	hypothesis	4	L4, U7
design	2	L1, U1	evaluate	2	L1, U10			
despite	4	**L3, U2**	eventual	8	L4, U3	identical	7	L4, U5
detect	8	L1, U6	evident	1	L4, U2	identify	1	L4, U2
deviate	8	L2, U8	evolve	5	L2, U7	ideology	7	L4, U6
device	9	L2, U3	exceed	6	L4, U1	ignorance	6	L2, U9
devote	9	**L3, U9**	exclude	3	L4, U7	illustrate	3	L4, U9
differentiate	7	L1, U4	exhibit	8	L2, U5	**image**	5	**L3, U5**
dimension	4	L4, U5	expand	5	L1, U7	immigrate	3	L2, U1
diminish	9	L4, U4	**expert**	6	**L3, U8**	impact	2	L1, U9
discrete	5	L2, U6	explicit	6	L1, U3	implement	4	L1, U2
discriminate	6	L1, U10	exploit	8	L1, U5	implicate	4	L4, U7
displace	8	L2, U7	export	1	L1, U3	implicit	8	L1, U3
display	6	**L3, U5**	**expose**	5	**L3, U5**	imply	3	L4, U7
dispose	7	L4, U6	external	5	L2, U10	impose	4	L1, U10
distinct	2	**L3, U7**	**extract**	7	**L3, U2**	incentive	6	L1, U10
distort	9	**L3, U6**				**incidence**	6	**L3, U10**
distribute	1	L4, U8	facilitate	5	L4, U1	incline	10	L1, U7
diverse	6	L2, U8	**factor**	1	**L3, U8**	income	1	L1, U3
document	3	L4, U9	feature	2	L4, U1	incorporate	6	L4, U4
domain	6	L2, U8	federal	6	L2, U3	index	6	L1, U4
domestic	4	L1, U3	fee	6	L1, U1	indicate	1	L2, U4
dominate	3	L1, U5	file	7	L4, U6	individual	1	L1, U1
draft	5	**L3, U6**	final	2	L4, U3	**induce**	8	**L3, U7**
drama	8	**L3, U5**	finance	1	L2, U2	inevitable	8	L2, U8
duration	9	L4, U1	finite	7	L1, U9	infer	7	L1, U8
dynamic	7	L1, U5	**flexible**	6	**L3, U9**	infrastructure	8	L4, U6
			fluctuate	8	L2, U7	inherent	9	L1, U1
economy	1	L1, U7	**focus**	2	**L3, U8**	inhibit	6	L1, U5
edit	6	L4, U8	format	9	L4, U8	**initial**	3	**L3, U7**
element	2	L4, U1	formula	1	L4, U8	initiate	6	L2, U10
eliminate	7	L2, U9	forthcoming	10	L4, U3	injure	2	L1, U1
emerge	4	L2, U1	found	9	L4, U8	innovate	7	L1, U3
emphasis	3	L2, U9	foundation	7	L4, U4	**input**	6	**L3, U6**
empirical	7	**L3, U4**	framework	3	L1, U1	insert	7	L2, U9

Word	Sublist	Location	Word	Sublist	Location	Word	Sublist	Location
insight	9	**L3, U7**	medical	5	L1, U2	percent	1	L2, U10
inspect	8	**L3, U3**	medium	9	L2, U2	period	1	L2, U6
instance	3	L1, U6	mental	5	L2, U6	persist	10	L2, U4
institute	2	L2, U8	method	1	L4, U9	**perspective**	5	**L3, U2**
instruct	6	L4, U2	**migrate**	6	**L3, U2**	phase	4	L1, U8
integral	9	L1, U4	military	9	L1, U4	phenomenon	7	L2, U5
integrate	4	L2, U7	minimal	9	L2, U10	philosophy	3	L4, U5
integrity	10	**L3, U7**	minimize	8	L1, U1	physical	3	L4, U4
intelligence	6	**L3, U8**	minimum	6	L4, U5	plus	8	L4, U5
intense	8	L1, U2	ministry	6	L1, U2	**policy**	1	**L3, U3**
interact	3	L1, U8	**minor**	3	**L3, U7**	**portion**	9	**L3, U9**
intermediate	9	L2, U7	mode	7	L4, U7	**pose**	10	**L3, U1**
internal	4	**L3, U7**	modify	5	L2, U3	positive	2	L1, U5
interpret	1	**L3, U3**	monitor	5	L2, U3	potential	2	L4, U8
interval	6	L2, U5	motive	6	L1, U6	practitioner	8	L1, U2
intervene	7	L2, U8	**mutual**	9	**L3, U3**	precede	6	L2, U4
intrinsic	10	L4, U4				**precise**	5	**L3, U10**
invest	2	L2, U4	negate	3	L4, U2	predict	4	L2, U1
investigate	4	L4, U8	**network**	5	**L3, U2**	predominant	8	L1, U8
invoke	10	L1, U3	neutral	6	L2, U10	preliminary	9	L4, U1
involve	1	L2, U3	nevertheless	6	L4, U10	presume	6	L2, U2
isolate	7	**L3, U4**	nonetheless	10	L4, U7	previous	2	L2, U5
issue	1	L4, U2	norm	9	L4, U6	primary	2	L1, U1
item	2	**L3, U10**	**normal**	2	**L3, U8**	prime	5	L4, U4
			notion	5	L4, U9	principal	4	L4, U5
job	4	L1, U1	notwithstanding	10	L2, U1	**principle**	1	**L3, U9**
journal	2	L2, U6	nuclear	8	L2, U7	**prior**	4	**L3, U6**
justify	3	L2, U3				priority	7	L1, U2
			objective	5	L1, U10	proceed	1	L4, U9
label	4	L2, U2	**obtain**	2	**L3, U6**	process	1	L1, U9
labor	1	L1, U2	**obvious**	4	**L3, U7**	professional	4	L1, U5
layer	3	**L3, U4**	occupy	4	L1, U9	**prohibit**	7	**L3, U10**
lecture	6	L4, U2	occur	1	L1, U2	project	4	L4, U4,U9
legal	1	L2, U3	odd	10	L1, U8	promote	4	L2, U6
legislate	1	**L3, U3**	offset	8	L4, U8	proportion	3	L1, U10
levy	10	L2, U9	**ongoing**	10	**L3, U3**	prospect	8	L2, U6
liberal	5	L2, U1	option	4	L4, U7	protocol	9	L2, U4
license	5	**L3, U9**	orient	5	L2, U5	psychology	5	L4, U2
likewise	10	L4, U5	**outcome**	3	**L3, U4**	**publication**	7	**L3, U1**
link	3	L1, U8	output	4	L1, U7	publish	3	L1, U3
locate	3	L2, U1	overall	4	L2, U6	purchase	2	L2, U9
logic	5	L1, U6	overlap	9	L1, U7	**pursue**	5	**L3, U8**
			overseas	6	L1, U1			
maintain	2	L4, U1				**qualitative**	9	**L3, U9**
major	1	**L3, U2**	panel	10	L1, U6	quote	7	L4, U10
manipulate	8	L4, U4	paradigm	7	L2, U6			
manual	9	**L3, U10**	**paragraph**	8	**L3, U6**	radical	8	**L3, U4**
margin	5	L4, U3	**parallel**	4	**L3, U9**	random	8	L2, U7
mature	9	L1, U8	parameter	4	L4, U5	**range**	2	**L3, U1**
maximize	3	L2, U8	participate	2	L1, U8	ratio	5	L1, U8
mechanism	4	**L3, U9**	**partner**	3	**L3, U1**	**rational**	6	**L3, U3**
media	7	L1, U5	passive	9	L2, U8	react	3	L2, U6
mediate	9	L4, U2	perceive	2	L2, U9	**recover**	6	**L3, U4**

Word	Sublist	Location	Word	Sublist	Location	Word	Sublist	Location
refine	9	L4, U4	specific	1	L1, U6	ultimate	7	L1, U9
regime	4	L2, U10	specify	3	L4, U6	undergo	10	L4, U1
region	**2**	**L3, U1**	**sphere**	**9**	**L3, U7**	underlie	6	L4, U6
register	3	L2, U2	stable	5	L4, U5	undertake	4	L2, U3
regulate	**2**	**L3, U6**	statistic	4	L4, U7	**uniform**	**8**	**L3, U1**
reinforce	8	L2, U5	**status**	**4**	**L3, U2**	unify	9	L4, U5
reject	5	L1, U7	**straightforward**	**10**	**L3, U4**	unique	7	L2, U1
relax	9	L1, U8	strategy	2	L2, U5	**utilize**	**6**	**L3, U8**
release	7	L4, U1	stress	4	L4, U4			
relevant	2	L4, U8	structure	1	L2, U1	valid	3	L4, U10
reluctance	10	L2, U4	style	5	L1, U4	**vary**	**1**	**L3, U10**
rely	**3**	**L3, U2**	submit	7	L2, U9	vehicle	8	L4, U3
remove	**3**	**L3, U2**	subordinate	9	L4, U3	**version**	**5**	**L3, U5**
require	1	L4, U2	subsequent	4	L1, U1	via	8	L1, U4
research	1	L4, U2	subsidy	6	L2, U2	**violate**	**9**	**L3, U6**
reside	2	L1, U2	substitute	5	L1, U1	virtual	8	L2, U10
resolve	**4**	**L3, U4**	successor	7	L2, U9	**visible**	**7**	**L3, U5**
resource	**2**	**L3, U8**	sufficient	3	L2, U10	vision	9	L4, U3
respond	1	L4, U7	sum	4	L1, U10	**visual**	**8**	**L3, U7**
restore	**8**	**L3, U5**	summary	4	L2, U10	volume	3	L2, U4
restrain	9	L2, U7	supplement	9	L4, U10	voluntary	7	L1, U10
restrict	2	L2, U9	survey	2	L1, U3			
retain	4	L4, U3	**survive**	**7**	**L3, U2**	welfare	5	L4, U1
reveal	**6**	**L3, U8**	suspend	9	L1, U10	whereas	5	L4, U2
revenue	5	L2, U2	sustain	5	L2, U4	whereby	10	L1, U4
reverse	7	L2, U7	symbol	5	L2, U2	widespread	8	L4, U10
revise	**8**	**L3, U6**						
revolution	9	L1, U1	tape	6	L1, U6			
rigid	9	L2, U7	**target**	**5**	**L3, U10**			
role	1	L1, U5	task	3	L1, U8			
route	9	L2, U5	team	9	L2, U6			
			technical	3	L1, U6			
scenario	**9**	**L3, U7**	technique	3	L2, U1			
schedule	8	L4, U9	**technology**	**3**	**L3, U8**			
scheme	3	L4, U3	temporary	9	L1, U9			
scope	6	L4, U8	tense	8	L1, U10			
section	1	L2, U5	terminate	8	L1, U9			
sector	1	L1, U3	text	2	L2, U4			
secure	2	L4, U6	theme	8	L2, U2			
seek	2	L4, U3	theory	1	L4, U4			
select	**2**	**L3, U1**	thereby	8	L4, U3			
sequence	**3**	**L3, U5**	thesis	7	L4, U7			
series	**4**	**L3, U5**	**topic**	**7**	**L3, U3**			
sex	3	L1, U3	trace	6	L1, U9			
shift	3	L4, U9	**tradition**	**2**	**L3, U6**			
significant	**1**	**L3, U10**	transfer	2	L4, U1			
similar	1	L2, U1	transform	6	L2, U7			
simulate	**7**	**L3, U1**	**transit**	**5**	**L3, U5**			
site	2	L1, U6	transmit	7	L4, U4			
so-called	10	L2, U8	transport	6	L4, U10			
sole	7	L4, U1	trend	5	L4, U6			
somewhat	7	L1, U4	**trigger**	**9**	**L3, U7**			
source	**1**	**L3, U2**						